a BROTHER'S
LOVE

Finding His Footprints

Michael Deauville

xulon PRESS

A Brother's Love
Finding His Footprints
by Michael Deauville

Printed in the United States of America.
Edited by Xulon Press.

ISBN 9781498484923

www.xulonpress.com

Table of Contents

Part 1: My Family

Part 2: Growing up a Sibling to a Disabled Child

Dedication

To all the siblings of children with disabilities, both visible and
non-visible:
May you continue going forward with your life knowing that
there is a mighty God in control and that you are an inspiration to
the world.

To Katie and Robert.
Thank you for making me the luckiest brother in the world.

To my Mom and Dad.
Thank you for being the glue that has kept our family together, and
for being an inspiration in my life. I admire you both.
I love you!

Foreword

A number of years ago I was a little league baseball coach. All three of my sons played baseball, and I coached their teams as a way of sharing and creating life-long memories in their lives. One of the great gifts of coaching is the number of great kids and families you meet and become close friends with. One of those friends that stand out in my memory is Michael 'Mike' Deauville; the author of this amazing book you hold.

He stands out because of his attitude, quiet confidence and humility amongst his peers, who were busy trading insults and trying to "one up each other and be the coolest of cool. Mike was the one that always helped me with the coaching bag full of equipment that weighed about the same as the Empire State Building. Most kids tried to leave practice as fast as they could so as not to be drafted to help with the dreaded bag, but Mike never did.

Mike has a precious sister with severe disabilities who attended our weekly Young Life Capernaum club; a place of joy, laughter, and belonging for her and her friends. This was a place where she learned that God loves her and she is not a mistake, but a miracle of God's love. Mike began volunteering with us at his sister's club, although he serves in a greater role today. Here again, in this platform; I saw Mike shine with such patience, compassion and leadership, not only for his sister, but for all the other kids in that club as well. He stood out even amongst our leaders.

When I read Mike's moving account of being a sibling to his brother and sister whom both have disabilities; my eyes were opened wide to two things. The first is that I found out why Mike is 'Mike.' His character has been forged through suffering and learning to love in the most profound of ways from his sister and brother. Secondly, I understood more clearly than ever before that the most overlooked part of a family that is blessed with a loved one with a disability is the sibling who does not have a disability. I've been around young people with disabilities and their families for thirty-six years, and I can tell you that healthy siblings are often invisible in terms of their challenges.

Mike's book is a gift from God for siblings who have a loved one with a disability. If you are a sibling, this book will be an amazing source of healing and comfort. You will feel like you are sitting and talking with Mike over a nice, cold soda. If you are not a sibling, read through this to understand the story and find his universal messages; then get this book into the hands of a family touched by disability. They will thank you. If I could get this book into the hands of every family touched by disability; I would. Mike keeps it real–the joys, the challenges, and the struggles.

Mike is a leader, one who deeply influences others. I know God has given him a story to greatly help others in the same situation. Thank you, Mike, for the amazing young man you are. Read ahead friend, and be encouraged!

Appreciatively for all siblings who have a brother or sister with a disability,

Nick Palermo

A Letter to a Sibling

**I write this with compassion, in hopes that children and people
growing up with siblings with special needs
can find the beauty in each individual,
helping to create a society
which values all human life.**

Dear sibling of a disabled person,

You are probably why you have to be the only child in the world that is growing up in your situation. You might be questioning, "Why do I have to be the odd one out?"

I get it. I asked myself that very question numerous times while growing up. I just wanted to live a normal life; if normal existed at all. I would be lying to you if I told you that I had the answer to your questions, because I don't. What I do know is that you are in this life because you will make the world a better place from your experiences.

The reality of growing up with siblings with special needs can be tough to comprehend. Initially, there are thoughts of confusion, hatred, anger and sadness. I felt all of these feelings, if not more. It is completely normal. Living with a unique sibling is not an easy thing to understand as we have no reason as to why *WE* have to undergo these trying circumstances. We have been placed in a world different than that of our friends. The way your family lives and approaches their life will never be identical to how a family without a disabled child lives, but that is okay. You will be stronger, worldlier, and you will still be able to live a successful, fulfilling life.

The reality of having siblings with special needs exposes you to many experiences that many others may never be exposed to. You have attended physical therapy, occupational therapy, and doctors appointments with your sibling. You have witnessed behaviors, outbursts, and medical procedures you probably wish you would have never seen. After all of those encounters, you have learned to love unconditionally, and be grateful for the life you have been given.

Ultimately, you may aspire to help those others in our world that are in need.

Living your special life will make you cherish the little things your siblings can do. I remember one occasion where my sister snapped her fingers after a medical procedure. She was not able to snap in the recent past. This small, yet profound gesture was something to celebrate in our household. So take the little milestones in your life, and cherish each and every moment you possibly can.

Growing up with siblings with special needs will encourage you to try harder, because you have someone to please and make proud. It will make you love deeper, because you know what life can bring. You will do silly things you never dreamt of doing just because it will make your sibling laugh or smile. Take pride in this, as you will be a wave for the future.

My biggest message to you to take away is that you are not the only child going through the challenges of life with a disabled sibling. Many other children, just like you, are living with similar challenges. The challenges you are facing will make you a much stronger and tolerant person. Erase the ideas of what life is supposed to be like; the norms and expectations.

Your friend's families may seem "perfect," but know that no family is "perfect." All families have their challenges; your challenges just may be appear different. Find the courage to live life to the fullest of your family's capabilities, and appreciate your loved ones; it is then that you will find joy. Nelson Mandela once said, "Courage was not the absence of fear, but the triumph over it. The brave man is not he who does not feel afraid, but he who conquers that fear." Embrace and conquer your anger and fear, despite the difficult challenges you face; your siblings and parents cherish you and love you.

Living a life with siblings with special needs has many challenges. You may be scared and hurt because you will be judged, looked at strangely, and sometimes even ignored. While growing up, you will be required to be courageous and exemplify compassion when standing up for your sibling and demonstrating what you believe in. It takes courage to be yourself, when surrounded by others who do not relate to who you are. It takes courage to do what is right for your sibling, even when everyone looks at you strangely, not completely understanding your situation. So I say to you, find courage as you live your life. You will inherently develop compassion for others and fully embrace it as a gift from the Lord. Your life will become much more meaningful from the variety of experiences you have endured and conquered.

With Encouragement,
Michael Deauville
March 2016

Introduction

*E*very child dreams of growing up with energetic, loving siblings. Whether it is an older brother to play catch with, or a younger sister to swim with; children jump at the opportunity to have a sibling. Siblings provide never-ending love for one another. They act as your biggest rival, and your biggest fan. They are your teacher and mentor. Above all, they are your friend.

Renowned children's author Marc Brown once said, "Sometimes being a brother is even better than being a super hero!" The author describes the greatness of brotherhood, and he exemplifies the love siblings have for one another. In my life; I greatly relate to the aforementioned quote. Being a brother to my two siblings with special needs has been challenging, but extremely rewarding.

I am the younger brother to two amazing siblings. I am ten years younger than Robert, an avid sports fan whom has taught me the importance of being dedicated and passionate about things that are important in my life. I am five years younger than Katie; a beautiful, loving girl who has taught me to never give up on what I believe in. I could never have dreamt of the two amazing siblings I was blessed with, because there is something about them that makes them different from everyone else in this world. My siblings are mentally and physically disabled.

The love and compassion I feel for my siblings with special needs can be immense. The challenges we face together in life have made us very close. My siblings have taught me so much more about life than anybody else ever could. My siblings' lives have shaped my life for the better, and for that I am forever grateful.

Attacking life with two siblings with special needs is all I have ever known. Robert was born with an encephelocele, which is an out-pocketing of the brain, and Katie, at the age of seven, was diagnosed with Metachromatic Leukodystrophy. The lessons and messages I have been taught over the years could never have been learned had I not had siblings with special needs. Because of my siblings, I have learned to advocate for people in need, and raise my voice for what is right, even when it was not the "coolest" thing to do. I have been inspired to find the value in each and every person, and strive to create a future where all are loved and respected.

Life with two siblings with special needs has been a marathon. There have been high points where we celebrated and rejoiced, and there have been low points where we hugged and prayed. Through it all, my family's dedication and love for one another has propelled us forward. Nothing in my life was easy, but I believe that at end of every trial in life is a hidden blessing that we can all celebrate together.

Growing up, people often sympathized with me and asked me the questions as to how I coped with living with two siblings with special needs. I was known as "an inspiration," "a hero," and "a man amongst boys." Through all of this praise, people still wanted to know how I managed to live a happy and successful life. Time and time again, my stories and testimonies as to how I managed opened the eyes and hearts of people from all different backgrounds. High school senior's hearts were opened to see the worth of every human being. Young primary school kid's eyes were opened to noticing that bullying the girl in a wheelchair was mean. Police officers learned to not stereotype a mentally disabled adult as a threat to society, but in reality, an asset to society.

From my unique perspective, people often engaged and wanted to learn more through conversation. Well, here it is: *A Brother's Love* is the message I want to share with the world. My book is something that I believe everyone can relate to in one way or another. Whether you are a sibling to a brother who is disabled, a parent to a daughter who is disabled or any other compassionate, loving person, I strongly believe that you will be able to take away a new sense of love and motivation to continue your life and create a brighter tomorrow. I believe that by opening your eyes and hearts to my stories, you can work to create a world where all are dignified and loved.

Buckle up, and put your helmet on. The story that you are about to hear will make you cry, laugh, and smile out of pure joy. You may be alarmed by some of the memories, but know that they are just a part of this crazy journey we all call life.

Each of us will all be tested with various obstacles in our lives, but if we find God's footprints in all that we face; we too, will find our very own footprints and live a meaningful life. *A Brother's Love* is the story of how I found mine.

Part 1:

My Family

1

The Beginning

"I know in my heart that man is good, that what is right will always triumph, and there is purpose and worth to each and every life."
-Ronald Reagan

The clock struck 12 and my mom's test in her agricultural economics class was over. She grabbed her test off of her desk and walked it up to the front of the classroom where the teaching assistant was collecting all of the student's work. She handed it to the nice looking young man and briefly started up a conversation. They introduced themselves and then went on their separate ways. My mom, Mary, a senior studying nutrition from Saratoga, California, was enjoying her final year of college at UC Davis.

The oldest of three girls, and a member of Alpha Phi sorority at UC Davis; my mom enjoyed playing tennis, swimming, and doing things with her friends. She had transferred to UC Davis after finishing her first two years of college at Santa Clara University. Her final year was going well and she was finishing up her degree. She was ready to start the next chapter of her life.

The following week, my mom once again started talking to Lindsay, the teaching assistant, after class. Mary and Lindsay talked about economics and then later met up at his fraternity party. Lindsay, a fifth year Senior from Fresno, California, was finishing his last quarter and was getting ready to graduate. A brother in Kappa Alpha, and agricultural economics major; Lindsay enjoyed fishing, playing baseball, and spending time in the outdoors. The two later agreed to go out on a date, and spent their first date together at a restaurant in Davis. One date was not enough and the two began a budding romance.

My mom and dad dated for a few months and things started unfolding very nicely. They complemented each other. They lifted each other up in the downs, and celebrated together at the highs. They were the perfect pair. My parents dated a few months and for some crazy reason or another, my dad got the idea to go to my mom's dad to ask for his permission to have my mom's hand in marriage.

My dad drove to Carmel, California over the Thanksgiving weekend to talk with my grandfather, and after the two talked, my dad got my grandfather's approval. Excited, my dad purchased the perfect engagement ring and planned the perfect proposal by Putah Creek behind the UC Davis Library. After about a week my dad got down on one knee to ask my mom to love him for the rest of her life. Young and in love, she excitedly accepted. Finishing up their senior years and ready to get on with their lives; the young, happy couple went forward with planning the wedding.

The following months flew by as the newly graduated couple was now planning their wedding for the following fall. From flower arrangements to wedding invitations; the wedding planning process overwhelmed them for the following months. On September 14, 1985, my parents were married at Saratoga Federated Church in Saratoga, California. The church was filled with family and friends from the Bay Area and Fresno who wanted to be a part of the start of a new chapter in my parent's lives.

The wedding and reception was intimate, sweet vows were exchanged and the young couple was married and ready for their honeymoon. After their honeymoon at Lake Tahoe, my parents moved in together in San Jose, California where they both had jobs. Lindsay was getting his MBA from Santa Clara University. Life was beginning to take shape and the future was bright.

After moving into their apartment together and starting their lives as a married couple, my mom started feeling sick. She was just not feeling herself. She went to the doctor, had some tests done, and then it was revealed that she was pregnant! Young and in love, my parents were newly married and now expecting their first child. Mixed emotions ran over my parents as they ranged from excited to fearful. On one hand, they were excited to bring a new addition into the family and share the joys of a child, but on the other hand, they were anxious of the responsibilities of a new child.

The following months went by without a hitch. The pregnancy was smooth and my mom handled it quite well. Every check up with her obstetrician went great, and my mom was overjoyed, expecting to receive a healthy baby. Time and money went in to preparing the nursery for the new arrival, and after nine short months the time came for my parents to truly prepare for the arrival of their newborn child.

On June 21, 1986, my mom went into labor and my dad rushed her to the hospital. Both of my parents' families met them at the hospital shortly thereafter as they all waited for my dad to come out with the news of the newborn. Within an hour of getting to the hospital, Robert Lindsay Deauville was born at 11:56 pm. Exhausted, my parents were ready to see their new baby son.

After seeing him for the first time, it was obvious to both of my parents that something was wrong with him. The doctors and nurses took Robert away for a few minutes and then brought him back. My parents knew something was amiss, but didn't know how to react. Robert's head did not look like a "normal" baby's head, and my parents were extremely frightened.

The rear of Robert's head had a large, mushroom-like growth. The doctors called it an encephelocele. An encephelocele is a rare neural tubal defect which creates an out pocketing of the brain. The news was something to be gravely alarmed about. From mental retardation, to vision challenges, learning delays, and poor fine motor skills, nobody can accurately determine how an encephalocele is going to impact a child. My parents were greatly alarmed.

In addition to being born with an encephalocele; Robert had agenesis of the corpus callous, which meant he did not have the vital network of nerves to connect the right and left hemisphere of the brain. Therefore, the left hemisphere could not communicate with the right. Without this vital structure in the brain, individuals can live happy normal lives, or they can have severe cognitive, social, and developmental disorders. Robert's future was very unclear.

The diagnosis of my brother was heart-wrenching for my parents. Every ultrasound and evaluation had come back perfectly clear for my brother while my mom was pregnant. How could he have been born disabled? The question challenged my parents immensely, but they took on the challenge of the loving their new son and providing the best medical care they could for him.

Following my brother's birth; he was in need of immediate medical attention for the encephelocele on his head. My brother was taken to a Stanford neurosurgeon who could remove the encephelocele. The surgery to remove the encephalocele was necessary because without being protected by the skull, the exposed brain was subject to harm. Fortunately, Robert's encephelocele was an out pocketing of a non functional brain material that needed to be protected.

Performing the surgery and removing the growth was also very risky. Putting a young baby under anesthesia has many risks and complications. So the procedure was scheduled for when Robert was 8 weeks old. Because the encephelocele was near the visual cortex, a big risk of his going blind was possible. The brain is such a fragile part of the body, so any small, minor, error could be life-changing.

Despite the immense amount of risks involved, performing the surgery was the only option because Robert could not live a normal life with the growth still attached to his brain. When my brother was two months old, he was taken to Stanford University Medical Center, and was prepared for his major surgery.

The morning of my brother's surgery was filled with emotions. For one, my parents were extremely nervous. Would their baby boy come out of surgery blind? Would their baby boy come out alive? These questions plagued my parent's minds as they waited during the surgery. They were joined by their family as they waited for the completion of the surgery. Everyone was on pins and needles as they waited for the surgeon to come out of the operating room and deliver the news.

The long surgery seemed like a lifetime to my parents. The hands on the clock seemed like they were not moving at all. My father paced around the hospital lobby, while my mom held hands with her mom: she was a rock in times of crisis. The wait seemed like an eternity. Finally, after the completion of the surgery, the neurosurgeon came out to my parents with good news.

The surgery had been successful, and my brother's brain was responding to all of the tests; signaling that it was functioning correctly. The only concern was that they thought that he would be blind. In the recovery room when my mom was allowed to hold him for the first time after surgery, she looked into his eyes and immediately told the nurse that he could see. The nurse said that he was probably just responding to my mom's voice, but my mom's motherly instincts knew that he could see and that everything was going to be ok. My family was overjoyed. Robert had survived the very risky surgery, and now he was able to hopefully live with fewer complications.

The immediate years following the surgery would ultimately prove whether or not the brain of my brother was damaged in the surgery. Would Robert crawl? Would Robert walk? Would he talk? These questions could not immediately be answered, as time would only tell.

Robert continued to grow and thrive following the surgery. He was sleeping, eating, and doing everything a normal baby should do.

Many milestones came as my brother was crawling by 10 months, and walking by thirteen months. He was progressing like all normal babies do. By the time my brother turned a year and a half old, he could already bounce a basketball. Robert was supposed to live a fragile life where he was to be challenged in so many ways, but by his willpower and courage to do what his heart had set, he was defying the odds.

My mom took Robert to his pediatrician, Dr William Blair, whom also happened to be her second cousin. The words Dr. Blair used to encourage my mom on how to raise Robert are words that my family still lives by today. "Raise Robert as if he were any other normal child." The biggest lesson that Dr. Blair taught my mom was that despite the challenges that Robert was diagnosed with, my mom needed to engage my brother in everything that she would engage a "normal" child into.

Robert was exposed to everything any other young boy would do. For instance, he had regular play groups, went to museums, and even attended a Mulberry Pre-school. Robert had some fine motor, gross motor and visual challenges, but nonetheless he was doing what every other young boy was doing. He hit all the baby milestones, although he had a slight delay in hitting them. He was living life to the fullest. The poor diagnosis had caught my parents off guard when Robert was born, but now they knew of nothing different and were raising their precious baby boy the way they thought was best for a child who was just perfect in their eyes.

Once my mom and dad understood Robert's situation, they began their life as a happy family. My dad was working during the day as an accountant while simultaneously going to school at night to receive his MBA. My mom was raising my brother and doing everything that she could to give Robert the best childhood ever. She took him to speech, occupational therapy, and physical therapy twice a week as well as taking Robert to playgroups, the park, and enrolled Robert in community sports. Life was going great for all, and the hope for tomorrow was as high as ever.

Robert continued to thrive, and the time came for him to go to preschool. He went to Mulberry Preschool, which was a parent participation school, where he played every day with "normal" kids. Robert was thriving in this environment, despite having some developmental delays. He made friends, loved his teachers, and continued to learn social and academic skills. Raising a child with special needs is no easy task for first-time parents. My parents were young and caught off guard, but they took the challenge head on and loved every minute playing sports and reading to him.

After their obvious, initial concerns of having a second child; my parents decided that it was time to grow the family with the addition of another baby. Robert was doing well and thriving in a four day preschool, so my parents thought that there was no better time to bring a new addition into the family. Thus, on August 2nd of 1991, Kathryn Anne Deauville was born. Making people smile from ear to ear immediately after arriving into the world, Katie, as we would call her, was the perfect addition to the family.

Healthy as can be; Katie gave my parents a sigh of relief after her arrival. All the fears of having a second child disappeared and the family looked ahead to raising Katie with Robert in the perfect family environment. Life was good.

The growing family was doing what all young families do. My mom was a stay at home mom raising two young children, enriching their lives with the appropriate elements for healthy growth. Robert was playing basketball, soccer, and baseball in local youth leagues, and Katie was growing up, participating in pre-school and play groups.

The years went by and Robert was enrolled in a special education class in elementary school. He was now able to get services for vision, speech and occupational therapy in the school. My mom would soon be on the Parent Teacher Association, and volunteered many hours each week for the school. Katie finally started kindergarten, and Robert was in fifth grade.

The thoughts of the kids growing up saddened my parents, and so they wanted to add one more child to the family. They were happy with the life they had, but they thought the addition of one more could only enhance the family. On March 9, 1997, I, Michael John Deauville, was born while my dad and the doctor listened to basketball games on TV in the back ground. The family's beautiful baby boy had arrived, and the family was complete.

I arrived home to the open arms of an older brother and sister. I can't say I remember this, but from the stories I hear; Katie was like my second mom. She treated me better then all of her "babies" and jumped at every opportunity to feed me a bottle or rock me to sleep. She was the ultimate big sister who did everything in her power to make sure I was happy and content. Robert, on the other hand, was excited to have a little brother to play sports with and teach the ways of boyhood. My siblings were elated to have a younger brother.

The next months flew by. I was a healthy, happy baby hitting all of the milestones at the correct times, and Katie and Robert were doing well in school and their lives. Robert was still playing every sport possible, and Katie was now competing on the swim and soccer team. Katie loved participating in girl scouts, and enjoyed playing with her American Girls Dolls with all of her friends. All three of us were growing ever so fast, and our family was happy to have the life we had. We were ready to tackle whatever would come our way. We just did not know what the obstacle would be.

2

The Championship Game

"Children with disabilities are like butterflies with a broken wing. They are just as beautiful as all others, but they need help to spread their wings."

- Unknown

$\mathcal{I}$t was a Saturday morning as typical as could be. My father woke up early and had already drank a cup of coffee and read the news. My brother was awake playing his favorite Nintendo Sixty-Four game. My sister was getting dressed for her soccer game, and I was eating breakfast with my mom. This Saturday, though, we had to go to the soccer field.

After the conclusion of eating our breakfast and brushing our teeth, my family loaded into the station wagon and headed over to the soccer field. The park, located only a few blocks away from our home, was a common location for our family to be. My sister Katie, who was now seven, and my brother Robert, who was now twelve, often had activities and games at the park. We thought nothing different entering the park on that given day.

We arrived at the park, and my dad rushed Katie in her white soccer shirt and black shorts over to the team warm-ups. My mom pushed me in the stroller to the field, as I was only twenty months old and my brother rode his scooter around the park like a mad man. We soon found the perfect location on the grass to watch the game. My mom put down a blanket for us to sit on, as well as some toys and a bottle to keep me entertained.

The soccer game began and the teams were very evenly matched. One team would put on an attack, and the opposing team would quickly counter the attack with equal, if not more force and aggression. This led to girls falling on the ground, scraping knees and elbows, as well as the receiving of bumps and bruises brought on by the competitive game. About midway through the first half, a scoring opportunity came for Katie's team. It was a beautifully placed corner kick by Katie, and her teammate smacked the ball with force into the net for a dazzling goal.

The goal was celebrated with hugs and kisses, but not too long after Katie's team's goal, the opposing team drove down the field and tied up the score with a goal of their own. Many minutes of competitive play followed until the referee blew his whistle to stop the game for halftime. At the half, the score was tied 1-1.

Despite the girls saying that they all loved playing soccer, halftime proved that they equally enjoyed the orange slices and Capri Suns that were provided by a parent at each game. The girls ran to their bench as fast as they could and dove into the fruit and drinks. Amidst the mayhem of devouring the orange slices, the coaches elaborated on what the team did well in the first half, as well as what they needed to improve on for the second. The lessons were well intended, but I question whether or not the girls actually listened.

The oranges ran out, and the second half of the game began. Katie was playing forward, her favorite position. You could see her excitement and joy in the twinkle of her eye. The ball was kicked around numerous times between both teams, and no team seemed like they were ever going to score the winning goal. About half way through the second half, a light shone when Katie's team had a breakaway opportunity following a poor pass from the other team. Katie's teammate had the ball and was dribbling up the field. Katie, a smart athlete, ran towards the center to get herself in a position to be passed to. Her teammate delivered a beautifully placed ball over Katie's head, right in the direction with the net. All that was between Katie and the goal was the goalie. Katie went and trapped the ball and headed for the goal. She was dribbling and just about to kick when all of a sudden, our lives changed forever.

Katie attempted to kick the ball, but instead fell face first into the ground. She had lost all of her coordination and muscle function and just flopped to the ground. There was no pothole, a defenders leg, or any other item that could have made her fall. Her body simply dropped. Katie began to cry, not just because she had scraped her leg, but because she had no idea what her body was doing. She was in perfect position, and her body failed.

Sadly, this would not be the only occasion of Katie falling. Over the next few months, Katie started falling repeatedly on her left knee when playing on the school yard or running to her friend's house down the street. As soon as the wound would heal, she fell again and re-injured her knee. To this day, she has a scar on her left knee because that is the leg that always hit first when she fell.

Katie had been on the swim team the previous summer and had great swimming form. This summer, however, Katie had slowed down and her arms seemed very weak. My mom could not figure out what was going on.

The former star student was failing in school. The former social butterfly was turning isolated and introverted. The former all star athlete was uncoordinated. My mother talked to my grandmother about what Katie was experiencing, and she told my mom not to worry, but Katie was not Katie anymore. My grandmother assured my mom that Katie would be fine. My parents grew alarmed when Katie's teacher phoned home alarmed at Katie's difficulties. She was having trouble reading and writing, and eventually, had difficulty copying off the board. My parents had noticed Katie's struggles, but the teacher phoning home was the tipping point.

Alarmed with the new circumstances; my mom called our pediatrician to set up an appointment for Katie to be evaluated. The following day, my mom took Katie out of school and they went to see the doctor together. They arrived at the doctor's office and the doctor examined Katie thoroughly. After a complete examination, our pediatrician concluded that Katie was perfectly healthy. She was where she should be on all medical charts and tests, and the doctor was not sure why she was failing. For the time being, he thought she was fine; but she was not fine.

My dad was content with the doctor's findings. He believed that the doctor knew what was right and Katie was okay. My mom, on the other hand, was not satisfied with the results, but went home anyways. The next week went by. Katie kept falling, and her muscle spasms were more evident. This caused my parents even greater concern. My mom phoned our pediatrician and asked for a referral to a neurologist. She was convinced Katie might have a brain tumor because of her consistent falls.

My parents took Katie nervously to the neurologist. The neurologist did a thorough examination; all the while my mom was watching and thinking to herself that Katie was failing the exam. Her abilities had been going backwards. The neurologist concluded that Katie was fine. Insistent that his findings were not accurate, my mom requested that a MRI be completed. The doctor relented, and ordered the scan. My dad was nervous, and was actually mad at my mom for being so persistent in wanting an MRI.

Two days later, Katie was prepped for the MRI. During the scan, more pictures were added and my mom knew something was drastically wrong. The doctor said that he would call Friday if the MRI pictures showed something of concern. Friday came, and my parents sat by the telephone all day long waiting for the results. Minutes seemed like centuries, and my parents were very concerned. The hours ticked by, and the moon rose into the dark sky. The day had passed without a doctor's call.

The next few days passed by, and there was still no call by the following week. We were overjoyed with the emotion that Katie was free from something dangerous. We were living a normal life with confusion, but little concern. On Tuesday afternoon, the neurologist called and asked to see my mom and dad in the office. He told them that the radiologist had indeed found something on the MRI. The doctor had diagnosed Katie with Metachromatic Leukodystrophy (MLD), a genetic, degenerative disease.

People who are affected by MLD lack an enzyme in their blood called Arylsulfatase-A. Sulfatides build up in the white matter of the brain and the Central Nervous System causing demyelenation. Consequently, the brain and nerves have difficulty communicating. Blindness, stiffness, seizures, dementia, paralysis, and eventually death occur in the MLD patient. My mom and dad were devastated.

A formerly perfectly healthy girl was now diagnosed with a terminal illness that would end her life far too short.

My family spent the next few months digesting the news. Thoughts of anger, confusion, and sadness plagued everyone's minds. What options are there? Is there a cure? How could this happen to us? My mom recalls waking up every morning hoping she would wake up from the horrific nightmare. No, the nightmare was real and was not going to disappear. Mom was very stressed and had difficulty eating for a while. She kept going to Katie and Robert's school and volunteering, trying to keep herself busy and occupied during this crisis as she adjusted to the news. She found strength in being with other people.

Dad, too, was stressed. He managed to go to work every day and would come home and play with his little girl. She was always Daddy's little girl. My dad always said that he wished someone would just ask him how he was once in a while. Men at work tend not to talk to each other the way that women do, so he did not find as much support as he would have liked outside the home.

Trying to grasp the diagnosis and the disease, my family set out to do as much research on the disease as possible. Initially, the neurologist told my parents to stay off the internet while they were adjusting to the news. Once the shock was over, and they could wrap their head around things better, my parents, aunts, uncles, and grandparents all set out to learn as much as they could about the disease. They learned of different treatment options and risks, as well as the prognosis if no medical procedures were to be completed.

My grandfather, Larry Wray, researched and found a treatment; a Bone Marrow Transplant. Some MLD patients were finding it somewhat successful in extending the life of the patient. The idea was that the transplant would stop the progression of the disease in the central nervous system, but not in the peripheral nervous system. My parents were told that the next stage of the research was around the corner and there was a possible "blue sky," but not a cure.

My parents took these findings to the neurologist. He had heard of the treatment, and sought out an expert on the disease. His discoveries led him to Dr. William Krivit, a hematologist and oncologist at the University of Minnesota Medical Center. Despite MLD being very rare, Dr. Krivit was a leading practitioner of the disease. Phone consultations followed which led to the decision to go visit Dr. Krivit in Minnesota.

In October, my parents packed their suitcases and took my sister on a plane trip to Minnesota to discuss the possibilities of a bone marrow transplant (BMT). My brother and I stayed with my grandparents and aunts so that my parents could focus solely on Katie. My parents took a taxi from the airport and arrived at the hospital a short time later. My parents filled out medical forms and insurance papers in order to be registered in the hospital system. After the busy work, my parents and Katie were called back to visit the doctor.

Dr. Krivit reviewed the MRI and did an examination on his own. More tests were performed which included a lung functioning test, psychological test, nerve conduction test, and an EEG. After reviewing all of the information, he concluded that Katie was a good candidate for the bone marrow transplant. Dr. Krivit gave my family a few options. If they were to do nothing, Katie would rapidly digress with losing muscle function, the inability to drink and eat, and an overall body failure, which would result in an early death.

The second option also posed many risks, but the prognosis was more promising. This option was the bone marrow transplant. If a match were to be found, Katie could be a candidate. Because individuals with MLD lack an enzyme call Arylsulfatase-A, a bone marrow transplant would replace the enzyme in the body in hopes that it would slow down the progression of the disease and improve Katie's quality of life.

My parents learned of their options and decided to think about it for a few days. Bone marrow transplants are not easy procedures to go through. The chemotherapy and radiation are extremely hard on the body, and many people die of complications due to infections and graft versus host disease. My parents returned home to me and my brother and processed the news, constructing a plan of attack. The following week, my parents again called Dr. Krivit, but this time they informed him that they would like to go ahead and follow through with the transplant. They were ready to fight for my sister and give her a second chance at life.

Over the next few weeks, blood was taken from everyone in our family to find a bone marrow match. Nobody within the family was a good match, so Katie's type was put on the bone marrow registry. A 5 out of 6 match was found and the donor agreed to go through with the bone marrow donation! A big hurdle was accomplished. Many transplants are not successful because the body does not accept the donated bone marrow, and a rejection of the bone marrow could be fatal. Thus, the tests to find the best match were extremely important.

3

Twin Cities

"We must let go of the life we have planned,
so as to accept the one that is waiting for us."
- Joseph Campbell

eaving San Jose in January with a young family was not going to be an easy task for my parents. My dad was working full time and had to request a leave of absence. Blessed with a loving work community, my dad received paid leave for as long as he needed. This was a blessing for our family, as we would have financial support and insurance through a very trying time. We stayed in an apartment at the Ronald McDonald House, and I loved playing with the other kids and toys. My brother was in the sixth grade and it was the first year that the Ronald McDonald House had a pilot school, so Robert was able to attend school every day there.

Katie was taken out of school, to never again return to the regular education classroom. My mom, a stay-at-home mom, put her life on hold to do everything in her power to bring my sister back home, healthy. I was just shy of my second birthday by about two months.

We boarded our flight to Minnesota, a place that we would call home for the next few months. We hoped and prayed that we would all return home together after the transplant. On the flight to Minnesota, a moment of hope overcame my family. Katie had the window seat on the big Boeing-737, and kept her eyes out the window as the plane flew above the clouds. About halfway into the flight, Katie said something that my family will never forget: "I see angels. They are right over there. They are going to keep me safe."

My parents looked at each other in shock. They looked out the window and could not see the angels that Katie was claiming to see, but nonetheless they knew that they were there. For the first time my parents knew that Katie had angels watching over her and that everything was going to be ok. She, too, had a newfound solace that she was going to tackle the forthcoming challenge and safely return home to her family and friends.

We arrived in Minnesota on a cold, winter January day, and we were picked up at the airport by the Ronald McDonald House shuttle. My parents had applied to stay at the Ronald McDonald House during our stay in Minnesota, as it was a home away from home for many families experiencing lengthy stays at hospitals. The Ronald McDonald House was a new safe haven for my family, and the place where I would spend an immense amount of time. It was our new home. We made many lifelong friends at the house, and we developed a loving support group always fighting on our behalf.

We unpacked our bags at the Ronald McDonald House and settled in. The house, which consisted of bedrooms, a kitchen, indoor and outdoor play areas, and family rooms were overrun by many different families who were all battling varying life threatening diseases. The house was always fully staffed with volunteers and paid employees, and it was the place where we would learn to become very comfortable in our four month stay in Minnesota. My family enjoyed the final night together with everybody in the Ronald McDonald House together under one roof, as the next day Katie would be admitted into the hospital for what would be an uphill battle to try to save her life.

After running all required tests and procedures between my sister and her anonymous donor; Katie started the long and dangerous process of the bone marrow transplant. Katie's little seven year old body was put through total body radiation and chemotherapy to kill Katie's personal bone marrow.

My sister was poisoned so much that she was on the brink of death. The rigors of the chemotherapy and radiation left my sister in a terrible state. She was nauseated and complained of a lot of stomach pain. The once beautiful young blond girl was now a pale, hairless little girl. The hardest part of the process for Katie was losing her hair. Her hair started to fall out slowly and then it fell out in big chunks. That is when we had a party in the hospital room and shaved her head. We made it an event!

After destroying Katie's bone marrow through radiation and chemotherapy; Katie was ready to receive her new, healthy, bone marrow. The donor, a young man who did not wish to be identified, endured a procedure to give his healthy bone marrow to Katie. After the extraction of the bone marrow from the donors' back pelvis, the healthy bone marrow was flown to Minnesota and given to Katie by

IV. Our family and nurses celebrated when the bone marrow IV was hung because that meant life was being breathed back into Katie. There is hope that there will be a steady increase of white blood cells to prevent infection, and that there is no graft versus host disease, which may cause severe complications of rejection.

The next week or two were the most important weeks of the transplant. Would Katie's body accept the new bone marrow? Would her white blood cell count increase to a level where infection is not as much of a worry? During this time, my aunts, grandparents, and my parent's friend Pam visited us and cared for my brother and me. They took turns and visited us each for a week. They helped us find a sense of normalcy in a time of hardship.

I can honestly say that some of my fondest memories are of the playroom at the Ronald McDonald house. While my brother was at a school in Minnesota, my grandma and I would spend countless hours crawling on the floors of the playroom playing with blocks and a train set. I was in hog heaven. I remember a young boy that I met at the house named Isaiah. Isaiah was close to my age and he was battling leukemia. Despite his illness, though, he and I enjoyed playing countless hours with each other in the playhouse and playground when he was not in the hospital.

As I have said before, my brother Robert is an avid sports fan. While we were at the Ronald McDonald house, my brother was given the trip of a lifetime to a Minnesota Timberwolves game. The Ronald McDonald house provided the transportation and tickets for my brother and grandmother, and they enjoyed a fun night together at the game. My brother was able to meet All-Star Power Forward Kevin Durant, and later even received a basketball signed by many of the players on the Timberwolves. This little amenity the Ronald

McDonald house provided allowed my brother to have a special night where he was celebrated and he could forget about his difficult family life for a few hours. Robert felt the love and support through a very emotionally trying time. The Ronald McDonald house truly was a sanctuary of love for my family.

While we were in Minnesota, many people in San Jose gave so much to our family to help us get through this difficult time. From people watching over the house, to making sure that we felt the love from so far away, the amount of support our family received was unreal. Katie's classmates sent her cards and gifts, and her Girl Scout Group, the Daisies, made her a blanket that had a hand-made picture on it from each girl. Katie's elementary school even supported her with a fundraiser. It was amazing, how much people cared. I know my parents will forever be grateful.

A few weeks passed, and it turned out that Katie's body was indeed accepting the new bone marrow. The blood cell counts were multiplying successfully, and the future was looking bright. She did have some setbacks with fevers that kept her from leaving the hospital earlier, but over time, it looked like her port was causing the infections. Once the port was pulled and replaced by a PIC line, her fevers went away, and Katie was then allowed to join us at the Ronald McDonald house. She came "home" and recovered outside of the hospital setting. Katie was recovering well, and then one morning she awoke with a high fever. She was pale and overtaken by chills and sweats. My parents rushed Katie back to the hospital.

The doctors observed Katie, but they could not find a reason for a fever. This fever could not be diminished despite all of the doctors working tirelessly to solve it. This was a major setback in Katie's recovery. For the next two weeks, doctors fought to lower her temperature, but with little success.

During this stay in the hospital, I celebrated my second birthday in my sister's hospital room. My sister was still very fragile and ill, so we held a birthday party in her room. The nurses brought in a big, wooden Snoopy sign that said "Happy Birthday" and I got to open my birthday presents which included various types of construction trucks, books, and clothes. The nurses, doctors and my family all enjoyed sharing a piece of birthday cake together. My second birthday was filled with great love, and I would not have wanted it any other way.

The party may have been a moment to celebrate me, but the bigger picture that I like to reflect on is that this was the initiation of the celebration of me coming to terms with the responsibility of being my sister's guardian. In the near future, I would be picking toys up off the floor so Katie's wheel chair could get by, and opening doors so my mom and dad could push Katie through the door. My mom told me I did this naturally and without hesitation or resistance. I took on responsibility at a very young age and that has contributed to who I am today.

Finally after a few weeks, Katie's body fought off the fever. Katie was then allowed to return to the Ronald McDonald house, in hopes that she would never have to return to the hospital again. She came home with a PIC line in her arm, so my mom could give Katie her antibiotics and medications. For the next two months, we stayed in Minneapolis in hopes that Katie's health would continue to improve so we could return to our home in California.

Before we left, we kept ourselves busy with activities provided by the Ronald McDonald House. There was Bingo, outings to baseball games, and game nights. We also spent countless hours with our good friends, the Franks; supporting each other and trying to live normal lives together, as our loved ones recovered from their bone barrow transplant. We shared the top floor of the Ronald McDonald House. Each family had their own apartment and often met in the common area in between. We enjoyed every possible part of our last days in Minnesota because we wanted to make the best of the situation as possible.

After a four month stay in Minnesota, Katie was finally cleared to return home. We packed up our home away from home, and said our final goodbyes to our large Ronald McDonald Family. We wished everyone well and let them know that they would be truly be missed. We then departed for the airport, and headed home to our wonderful city of San Jose.

We arrived home to the love of friends and family and a big, "Welcome Home" banner on our garage. Everyone was so supportive and loving in a time when we needed it the most. Our everyday lives changed immensely when we returned back home from Minnesota. Robert went back to his school, but Katie was unable to return to hers. Katie spent the next seven months continuing to recover from the BMT. She was unable to go to school because her immune system was not strong enough yet, so the school sent a home school teacher to work with her a couple of hours a week, so she could keep up her skills.

We made frequent outings to Jamba Juice and Taco Bravo with my grandmother Sally, where Katie could get a treat for the day and we could sit outside away from other people's germs. We had to be careful not to be around people with colds, as not to transmit the sickness to Katie. So play dates and pre-school for me were non-existent for a few months post transplant.

People did come to visit us at our home, which lifted everyone's spirits, but they needed to be healthy. They were careful to wash their hands in order to keep germs away from Katie. We missed many family and social events due to someone having a cold, and Katie couldn't be around any illnesses. Katie had countless medications she needed to take and often she would throw them up, only to have to re-take them. Life was different, but it became the new normal.

In January, 2000, medically fragile and unable to walk; Katie was placed in an orthopedically impaired special education class which had physical therapy, occupational therapy, and speech therapy services. Katie's therapies helped her retain as much of her abilities as she could. Her life was turned upside down, but her attitude was as good as ever as she woke up each day ready to tackle the day ahead.

My dad slowly integrated back into the working lifestyle, and my mom tried to do as much as she could to give all three of her children the best life possible. The normal life as my family knew it was gone, but we could not dwell on the past and just had to look forward to our future and take life day by day, as nobody knew what to expect. We may have passed the most difficult series of events of Katie's battle, but the diagnoses and treatments were only the beginning of a very unique journey.

4

A Warrior from the Beginning

"My mission in life is not merely to survive, but to thrive; and
to do so with some passion, some compassion, some humor, and
some style."

- Maya Angelou

$\mathcal{T}$he youngest of three siblings; I was supposed to be the one
being taken care of by my older siblings. Soon, it was evident that I was going to be the most capable of the three. Between
Robert's poor fine motor skills and learning delays, and Katie's tragic

disease resulting in her becoming wheelchair bound; I was the only "normal" child. I realized this at a very young age. I did not know anything different, however; it was my world. I was the youngest child, but I would grow up giving and providing constantly for my siblings to the best of my ability.

Siblings of children with disabilities face a life vastly different than that of their peers. Nothing we encounter will be matched by anybody else. We mature far beyond our years due to the responsibilities we inherently take on at an early age, as soon as we are capable. We are unique individuals who develop a compassionate heart and understanding for others. With that being said, it is a different life we live which has many unique ups and downs. Many people are unable to empathize with you in certain situations and many people ignorantly say things that may be offensive. There are countless, everyday situations that siblings face that their peers will not.

My life has been the epitome of a life of a sibling of children with disabilities. I have observed and participated in many positive and negative experiences and ultimately learned from those experiences. I have also hurt inside and questioned, "Why do I have to be a part of this and everyone else has such a "normal" life?" I struggled to understand it all. It was the life I was given, and looking back, I would not change it for the world.

People with disabilities are the largest minority in the world in population. From autism to cerebral palsy, many different diseases and disorders affect millions of people worldwide. With these individuals, though, come their siblings. I, and many other siblings, faced the life of growing up with a disabled child. In my case, it was two siblings, but that just gave me a little extra love and appreciation for the life I am in.

The upcoming section of the book takes you on the journey of being a sibling of a disabled child. It takes you on an emotional rollercoaster of how I overcame the obstacles, and found solace. Many times in my life I have been in a situation where I did not understand the way I was feeling, but more importantly; I did not know who to ask for help. I thought I was all alone. Inspired to help others in my shoes, this book is meant to be a tool to help people better understand growing up with a disabled sibling. Despite the subject matter being very concrete, the lessons and morals can stretch out to help people understand and overcome any challenges they face.

I believe that there are many lessons in life that you cannot learn unless you experience a difficult situation. If you take that situation and look back at it after a few weeks, a few months, or a few years, you can apply what you have learned, and identify how it has helped you grow and become a better person. After doing so, you are able to look back, and say that you have gained valuable lifelong lessons that you could never have received anywhere else. As I share my story, I honestly believe that I have gained irreplaceable lessons that have made me a stronger, compassionate person.

A Brother's Love: Finding His Footprints takes you on the journey I experienced to understand the life of being a sibling to children with disabilities. The following chapters are how I overcame many of the difficult questions and situations in my life to find peace and meaning. Finding God's footprints in my life and my siblings' life enabled me to find the meaning for my existence. God's footprints gave me a profound amount of hope, as I believe that when you accept who you are, and are confident that you are the person God wants you to be; you can move forward in your life with a newfound purpose, a pure mind, and a heart filled with love. I may be the brother of two siblings with special needs, but I would not change it for the world, and I am proud to say it has made me the dedicated, compassionate person I am today.

This is my story.

Part 2:

Growing up a Sibling to a Disabled Child

5

This Does Not Make Sense

"He explained to me with great insistence that every question
possessed a power that did not lie in the answer."
- Elie Wiesel

We loaded the Euro van with the ski gear, and enthusi-
astically jumped into the car for the three hour ride to
the Boreal ski resort. My family, including my aunts and cousins,
drove to Tahoe to enjoy the fresh new snow. We caravanned up the

mountain and convened at the ski resort. I was filled with excitement because my cousins, both who are younger than me were finally old enough to ski the same slopes as the rest of us. We were all excited and ready for a great day on the mountain.

When we arrived at the ski resort, we put on our snow pants, jackets, helmets, and gloves, and carried our skis a short distance to the resort. My dad, who was with Katie, Robert and Aunt Lori; set up base at a picnic table on the deck of the resort. They pulled out books and cards and prepared for a day at the resort, while the rest of us skied. My mom and Aunt Lesley went to the ticket counter to buy our lift tickets, while my cousins, Natalie and Gracie and I put on our skis. After falling a few times with my glasses becoming foggy with steam, the tickets arrived and we were ready to hit the slopes!

The day went well, and we enjoyed great company as we tore up the snow. We rode the ski lift to the top of some intermediate level hills and the girls loved skiing down the steep hills. We had a fabulous time being together and sharing the great outdoors with each other. The time came for the last run of the day. We unanimously decided to choose the slope that was directly facing the resort. We took the chair lift up, and prepared for our final descent. When we reached the top, I looked down from the top of the mountain and saw the beautiful resort deck, where I then noticed my sister and brother sitting together watching us about to ski down the hill.

I immediately started reflecting on how lucky I was to be skiing. All my life I have been able to do so much more than my siblings. My poor sister and brother, enjoying themselves on the resort deck and not complaining, probably wishing they were capable of skiing. I stood on the top of the mountain that day, immersed with sadness and confusion. Why was I so lucky?

Right then and there I started reflecting on my life. Here I was on top of the mountain skiing, while my siblings were bound to just watching me from the deck. How was I fortunate enough to be skiing and they lacked the ability? Was this fair? I just could not understand why my sister and brother were bound to their constraints. I was dumbfounded.

The confusion I felt may be similar to how you feel when dealing with a major setback. In my life, living with siblings with special needs is very emotional. Beside the initial reaction of being completely shocked, mad, and sad; the biggest reaction I had was pure confusion. Growing up, I had to find a reason for all that was happening to my siblings. My inquisitive self wanted to get to the source of all of their struggles. I was full of questions.

For so many people, including myself, a diagnosis of disabilities poses two huge questions: "Why is any of this happening?" and, "Why is this happening to me?"

These very questions floated through my head while I tried to get an understanding of my siblings' lives. As a young child, I had a small understanding of life. I had no understanding of fate, and I had very little understanding of disease. Thus, I could not answer any of my questions. Confusion prevailed in my mind. I remember numerous times asking my parents why this was happening. To my dismay, it seemed like every time I asked, I received a different answer. "It is just life." "It's all a part of a plan." I still was not content with the answers.

My intuition to learn as to why all of this was happening led me to the internet. Growing up, I researched about my siblings diseases. I learned as much as possible, in hopes that maybe I would find reason for how everything was unfolding. Similarly, I remember that each doctor's appointment, physical therapy session or other meeting that my parents took my siblings to; I tagged along in hopes that a groundbreaking term would be said that would give me the reason for everything.

Through my internet research, I found the scientific reasoning for both their diseases. My sister was stricken by her disease because my parents both carried a gene which, when joined together, through the magic of creation; gave each offspring a twenty-five percent chance of being diagnosed with MLD. It was a recessive genetic disorder. (Like that made any sense to me at the age of 5.) Similarly, my brother was afflicted with his disability just because it was a risk that arrived with any pregnancy. Despite this knowledge, I still had no reason as for *why* my siblings had to suffer with their disabilities. I had the scientific reasoning, but I did not have the real answer. Was there a greater power who wanted this? Had my siblings done something to deserve this? I had no idea.

I took my scientific reasoning to friends and family, but still longed for the philosophical reasoning which would provide some closure on my confusion. Time and time again, though, I was given the phrase, "Everything happens for a reason." I hated that! How could one put a reason for a young innocent baby boy being stripped of a normal life before he even had a chance? That is unexplainable. Similarly, how could one put a reason behind a young energetic girl being robbed of her freedom and permanently placed in a wheelchair at the age of seven? That the smart, athletic seven year-old was given a death sentence? No reason for any of this exists, and I simply could not cope with the response I was given far too often.

I remember one occasion during elementary school when my sister fell very ill with pneumonia. She had developed a high fever, and was very sick. She was taken to the hospital for a few days, and my brother and I stayed with my aunt and uncle for a few days. I remember lying in bed, unable to sleep, thinking about my sister. My sister had already suffered immensely in her life, so why did she have to take on another fight? I had never faced a serious illness, yet my sister kept on being victimized. I was confused as to why she had to continuously get sick. I did not understand any of it. It was not fair.

Time and time again, my siblings' lives provided me great confusion. I was a young boy when all of these thoughts began to cross my mind, so I could not answer most of the questions that I had. Even as I grew older, I still was unsure as to why my sibling's challenges existed. Difficult situations pose us many questions. More often than not, we are unable to find our answers.

Living with siblings with special needs is very challenging at times. When diagnoses are originally made, everybody has questions and concerns. Despite all being determined to find answers, siblings of kids with disabilities have an especially hard time because they are usually very young, and have little reasoning on life. Being a young sibling, I too was left unsure. I spent many nights lying wide awake just simply confused. I made my family aware of my concerns, however and they helped me every step of the way. The answers I received frequently left me unsure, but through the love and support of my loved ones; I was encouraged to move forward.

Questions and confusion are innate human reactions when we face unfamiliar situations. Today, society preaches knowledge and the importance of finding answers to everything. So, when we cannot find answers, we search for them. Sadly though, many questions that siblings have about their siblings' difficulties go unanswered or are not fully understood. When the questions persist, confusion prevails.

Having siblings with special needs will pose many questions, and the confusion incurred is all a part of growing up in the situation. It is a part of the acceptance process. There are limitations to human inquiry, so it is ok to not know all of life's answers immediately.

6

What about Me?

"You can be the moon and still be jealous of the stars."
- Gary Allan

$\mathcal{P}$eople tend to like getting all of the attention. They like to be in the spotlight of all activity. Being a sibling of a child with disabilities, I was no different. Especially being the youngest child; I hoped for all of the attention in the world. From grandparents to strangers, I wanted to be the center focus. Sadly, that dream was short lived. I often was not the center of attention. I believe that is the case with siblings of children with disabilities as well.

Being the secondary focus can be hard for young children to understand while growing up. It is sometimes impossible to fathom why you are not receiving the same exact attention as that of your siblings with special needs. It is the truth, and as selfish as it sounds, it often times leads to jealousy on the "normal" sibling's behalf.

One summer, my entire family and I took a vacation to visit my aunt, uncle, cousins and extended family in Washington D.C. My cousins did not live directly in the city, but we stayed with them in their home in Virginia and toured our nation's capital for a little over a week. We enjoyed touring all of the Smithsonian Museums and monuments, but a pivotal moment came when we went to the Hart Senate Building to get prepared for our tour of the United States Capitol Building. When we arrived to Senator Dianne Feinstein's office, we were greeted by her aides who briefed us on the visit, and handed us the papers needed for our tour. Before we departed for the tour of the Capitol Building, we were unexpectedly greeted by Senator Feinstein.

She had just finished a meeting with her colleagues, and she was returning to her office for afternoon work. When she saw my family, she came rushing over to introduce herself and learn a little bit about our unique family. She asked where we were from, how we were enjoying our stay in Washington, and even what illness my sister, Katie, had.

My family spoke with the Senator for a good ten minutes, and at the end, she told us to wait outside of her office for her to return. She went into her office, and gathered two coffee cups which she had painted, as well as a United States Senate blanket which she gave to my sister. Intrigued by our story, Senator Feinstein wanted to spoil Katie a little bit before we left on our tour. It was a thoughtful act, and to this day, I have the Senate blanket hanging in my room and we still have the mugs displayed in our house. We were humbled by her kindness to our family.

To say I was jealous would be an understatement. I was not jealous of the coffee mugs, or even the blanket, but I was jealous because I received very little attention in the meeting. I spent the entire conversation as a bystander. I was by no means the topic of discussion, nor were any of the gifts directly presented to me. Who knows if I was even recognized?

You may think that I am sounding selfish right now, but the situation which I just described is very frequent event to being a sibling to children with special needs. I was jealous of all of the attention my sister Katie received. I wanted to be the one receiving special gifts, not watching my sister receive them.

Growing up with siblings with special needs, I constantly faced situations where I was a bystander. This created jealousy. I was by no means jealous of my siblings' disabilities, but I was jealous of the attention they received from having special needs. Time and time again, my siblings received various gifts and praise from people, while I silently stood listening to the words. This was hard. At one moment you are happy for your siblings, but at the same time you cringe at the idea that they are getting something and you are not. Being a young child, I could not fathom being unnoticed, and to this day, I recount stories far too similar to what I described where I did not receive equal notice.

Similar occasions occurred every time my family and I went to Disneyland. On each visit the characters and staff payed extra attention to my siblings. From being able to cut the lines to the front to getting extra-special visits from Disney characters; my siblings received special arrangements while I did not. Being with my family, I too reaped some of the benefits, but the realization that we were getting the benefits because of my siblings and not myself made me jealous.

I wanted to be a positive contributor to my family, but instead I felt I was just a side-bag following along as my siblings brought in more attention. It was great for my siblings to get the attention, and I am glad that they were able to receive some time of fun and happiness, but being a young boy with a desire to please; I was jealous of the attention that I was not getting. I just wanted to get some of the recognition from all of the cool people who gave special attention to my siblings.

Besides being jealous of strangers and celebrities giving more attention to my siblings than myself; I too experienced the jealousy of my parents devoting more attention to my siblings. Because of my siblings' needs, my parents gave them extra help and care all of the time. From helping them do many daily activities such as tying shoes, bathing, helping them dress, and feeding Katie, my parents gave my siblings extra attention. I remember coming home from school every day, and when I got home; I was met with my mom helping my sister get off of the bus and feeding her a snack.

I knew that my sister needed the help, but at the same time, I just wanted to be the center focus. At home, my mom fed my sister snacks, and I often went into the kitchen and chose my own snack.

I longed to be served by my mother, but instead I often times had to fend for myself because I was capable of doing it. By no means was my mom inattentive to me, but because of my siblings' special needs, I often times had to fend for myself to get what I wanted.

Jealousy did not stop there. Similar to the jealousy I felt from my siblings getting extra attention, I too felt jealous about the lives my friends were leading. I had no friends who had siblings with special needs. All of my friends were either an only child, or they had "normal" siblings. Their lifestyles seemed so normal, and I was envious. Parents frequently punish their children for wrestling and fighting with each other, but I would have done anything to have been able to be terrorized by my sisters Barbie's, or fought my brother over the biggest piece of birthday cake.

Gary Allan's quote accurately explains how one can be jealous of another even when they are not in a bad situation of their own: "We live in a world of envy, and even when our lives are okay, we often times feel jealous of others." This quote precisely describes the way I felt. I absolutely loved Katie, Robert, and my parents, but despite my love for them, I still was jealous because I felt that the extra care my siblings received was taking away from the attention I wanted from my parents. I did not wish my siblings to have anything bad happen to them, but sadly, jealous thoughts persisted in my head.

Jealousy is an innate response in the human life. It is a natural instinct when we see something that we want. Growing up with siblings with special needs, one often finds themselves second in mind. They are frequently in positions where they are simply overlooked. It is not that their loved ones and strangers do not love them equally as much, but it is because their siblings require extra care. Thus, they obtain that extra-special recognition and time.

For me, it was hard to comprehend why this inequity existed, and I believe that other siblings feel the same. Siblings of children with special needs face special circumstances in their lives, and the occurrence of not occasionally being the center of attention leads to many siblings' feeling jealous of their friends and siblings. Jealousy can be stubborn in many occasions, but nonetheless it is frequently felt while growing up with siblings with special needs.

When jealousy of others and your siblings exists, it is important to find a meaning for it, and to find a way to overcome it. Many times in my life I felt jealous, and I had a difficult time trying to conquer the feeling. I tried so hard not to feel the emotion, but it seemed as though every time I tried not to feel it; I felt it more. If I could just get over this feeling, I could live more freely. By being restrained by jealousy and unable to feel like the attention was on me; I often would do things on my own simply because I knew that it didn't require anybody else. Further, I would just try and put aside my siblings' challenges and focus on myself as I just wanted everything to be ok. By being jealous of my siblings' extra attention, I was challenged to be more independent and do things for myself as I thought my siblings would get all of the attention anyway.

It is easy to be jealousy of others. It is easy to not be content with what we have. At the same time, it is possible to understand that we are in the plan of someone else. If we can understand that we have a future full of prosperity and hope, we can feel comfortable with all that we have.

There were times in my life where I envied others. Even today, I see people who seem like they just have everything going right. How could I not be jealous? Through the challenge of understanding that I was going to have a life full of greatness just like the others;

I was able to feel satisfied with my life. We all long for what we do not have, but if we understand that we will live a life full of richness, we can accept and love the great life we have been given. I may have been jealous in many different situations, but I realized that I had so much to be happy with in the wonderful siblings I have. Katie and Robert are such gifts and they provide so much good in my life. They have done the unthinkable time and time again, and they have inspired me to be a better person. If anything, I should be jealous of all the lives they have touched, not the extra attention they have received.

7

Just laugh at it, its life!

"Remembering that I'll be dead soon is the most important tool I've ever encountered to help me make the big choices in life. Because almost everything–all external expectations, all pride, all fear of embarrassment or failure–these things just fall away in the face of death, leaving only what is truly important."

- Steve Jobs

We packed into the auditorium after a delicious dinner in San Francisco and sat down to watch the San Francisco Symphony perform. My dad had purchased tickets for my family to take my mom to the symphony for Valentine's Day. After finding our seats and sitting down, the ensemble came onto the stage and started their act. Playing many famous pieces from Mozart, the orchestra blew the audience away with their accuracy and strength. They were truly phenomenal. I am no expert musician, but if you ask me, they did not miss a note, not like I would have known if they did anyways.

A few songs into the show, Katie, who was sitting between me and my dad, started making some noises of laughter. She was obviously enjoying the show, and the way she could present it was through the noises she made. Sadly, the symphony was no place for noise. When all were quiet, one could hear a pin drop, and when Katie laughed, her noise filled the area. Every person surrounding us in their seats immediately turned to look at us.

We received some dirty looks from people who were probably season ticket holders, and when noticing who the noise was coming from, the irritated folks still did not seem to care. They were annoyed, and probably wished we were not there. The looks of all the people made me sad and angry, but above all; I was simply embarrassed. Katie, who could not control any of her sounds and emotions, made people annoyed. She quickly settled down after my mom and dad quieted her. I sat in embarrassment as I watched the rest of the show.

Having siblings with special needs poses many emotions which conquer a child's life. One of the most significant emotions though, is the feeling of embarrassment. Growing up, siblings are going to feel embarrassed repeatedly, and it is all a part of the process of acceptance. Embarrassing situations will frequently arise, and the feelings will persist in various settings as your life goes on.

I remember a time in grade school when I was assigned a group project. I am sure, you too, can relate to being assigned group work while in school. Anyway, I was assigned a group which consisted of me and one of my school friends. We were excited to be partners, and we talked to our moms to set up a time to meet for the building of the project. The week passed on, and Friday arrived. My mom was waiting in the car, and my friend and I walked out to greet her and go home to work on the project.

When we arrived home, we were greeted by a bright yellow school bus in which my sister was inside. When we hopped out of the car, we were greeted by something alarming. Katie was crying hysterically. For anybody who does not know Katie, they would be greatly concerned at this occasion. Being her brother; I knew exactly why Katie was crying. It was a hot day, and because of Katie's disease, her body cannot regulate temperature like everybody else. Thus, her muscles start spasming and she ends up in a great deal of pain. It requires cool air, water and Ativan to help calm her muscle down.

When my friend noticed the situation, he immediately froze. He had no idea as to why Katie was crying, nor did he feel comfortable being in the situation. As soon as we walked inside the house, my friend asked for the phone. He called his mom to come pick him up. He was uncomfortable being around Katie, and thus did not want to be my partner for the project. From that day on, my friend never looked at me the same way again. Again, I felt embarrassed and isolated again from my friends.

I grew up knowing nothing else than having siblings with special needs. Little did I know that very few people in our world actually have to deal with the difficulties that I did while growing up with my two siblings. The aforementioned story was a pivotal moment for me growing up. For the first time, I lost a friend because of one of my siblings. He had no idea who my siblings were before that day, and after noticing who I lived with, he decided that we could no longer be friends.

This occurrence led me into a stage of embarrassment of my siblings around my friends. For a long time thereafter, and sometimes even to this day, I feel shy about introducing new friends into my home because I am simply embarrassed and worried that my friends will not view me the same way because of my siblings' limitations. I was always eager to go to a friend's house, but at the same time, I dreaded the idea of having friends over to my house. I just wanted to be viewed for who I was, and not for who my siblings were. Sadly, many people in our society are not comfortable with children with special needs, and thus do not give them the compassion and love they deserve.

My embarrassment led me to be shy around new friends, and it probably ultimately led me to seek out certain individuals who I thought might be more understanding. After devoting myself to my own needs of friendship and companionship; I did find friends who accepted me for who I was, and did not label me for having siblings with special needs.

If you are a sibling of a child with disabilities, I can almost guarantee you that you are going to find yourself in a similar situation as to the one I just described. Because of how our society teaches, many people's hearts are not open to different types of people. This results in many people being closed off to the idea of viewing people with noticeable differences as equal counterparts. People then begin to feel uncomfortable, and as we all know too well; this results in people just turning the other way.

Because of people's lack of acceptance, embarrassment is a common emotion. You will be embarrassed in front of your friends, and maybe even in front of strangers, but know that you are not alone in these feelings. Further, do not let it keep you down. If you are embarrassed and unsure of how your friends will react, find friends who can accept you for who you are and for who your siblings are. These loving, accepting people exist in our world, and I was very fortunate to find some in middle school and beyond.

Even after finding a community who can accept you for who you are, you will find situations when people still make you embarrassed for having siblings with special needs. One night, my brother, who loves sports, wanted to go to my high school's basketball game. I decided that I would take him with me. When we got to the game, he did his own thing, and I stood by some friends. About a quarter the way through the game, I grabbed my camera to take some pictures for my art class.

I left the bleachers, and headed over to an open area where I could stand and snap a few shots. As I was taking pictures, I overheard two police officers joking about a man in the stands. They were laughing and saying some rude comments, and even throwing in some "police code words." Concerned about whom they were making fun of, I looked up and noticed that they were making fun of my brother. I immediately opened my phone and Googled up some of the code words they were saying, such as the term "51-50." After reading a few lines, I learned that the term correlated to an individual who is mentally unstable and a threat to the community. I was heartbroken.

These police officers, whom are supposed to protect those in need, were verbally assaulting my brother and laughing about it.

I wasn't sure what to do. Should I just let it slide like I have done so many times before? Or, do I tell the police officers how I really feel? I wasn't sure, but decided to follow my gut and call them out. I approached the two officers and asked them what the term 51-50 meant. When they did not respond to my question; I told them that I understood everything that they just said, and that the person they were joking about was my brother. Both of the officers' jaws dropped like I have never seen before. They were in shock and embarrassed. I continued to tell them that the man they were making fun of has developmental disabilities, and that the only threat he was to society was teaching them how to love one another for who they are on the inside. I left it at that, and went back to my seat.

After returning to my seat; I was greeted by some supervisors and school officials, trying to create a happy resolution. I told them that it was not a big deal, and we moved on. Oh but, it was a big deal, I was embarrassed and in shock. How could a police officer do such a thing to a vulnerable member of the community? It has nothing to do with the profession itself, but the individuals were obviously not feeling any concern or love to my innocent brother. I was embarrassed for my brother because he did not deserve to be spoken poorly about, and because he was unable to defend himself. I was embarrassed that two people could willingly do such a thing to another human being.

I heard so many harsh comments and jokes about my siblings while growing up. I was embarrassed and sad though, because I knew that my siblings could not speak up for themselves. People do not feel any sympathy for people in need, and they do not understand what effect their harsh words have on others. Having encountered numerous situations where I overheard people degrade my siblings; I have become calloused to the harsh comments, but nonetheless embarrassed that people can be so cruel. I have found that pride and a strong shoulder can help you navigate through the rough waters.

As we grow up, we are going to reach the time when dating and interacting with significant others becomes a part of our life. During my junior year of high school, I met a very nice girl at a conference in Carmel. After a few conversations, I asked her out to a basketball game at my school. She said yes, and we went to the game and had a great time. I took her home, and we both agreed to hang out again soon.

A couple weeks passed and we hung out quite a bit, and by then it was, as the cool kids like to call it; "Facebook Official." She and I were dating. We went on some fun dates to different places, but even after a few weeks, my mom had still not met her. My mom kept bugging me to bring her over, constantly giving me a hard time about not bringing her around. In fact, I did not want my girlfriend to be scared away by Katie and Robert. I liked this girl so much and I did not want to feel the heartbreak of losing her because of my siblings.

I decided that I should talk to my girlfriend about my family situation, and so I did. After she assured me that it would not be a deal breaker, she and I went over to my house one night and she met my mom and sister, who at the time; were the only ones home. It could not have gone any better. My girlfriend was very comfortable around my sister, and although there was an obvious timidity, she stuck it out like a champ, and I am forever grateful.

As siblings come to terms with dating and having relationships with other people, the constant question of, "Will she still date me?" exists. Siblings of children with disabilities face a unique situation when it comes to this. Many times it can be embarrassing to introduce a girl to the family, but put in siblings with special needs and it is taken to an entirely new level. Siblings face the enormous battle of finding significant others who accept the situation for what it is, and feel comfortable around the entire family.

I have thought about the day for as long as I can remember, but I am confident that there are people in this world who will feel perfectly comfortable and content in the situation. I have met some amazing young women in my life who have shown me that love has no boundaries and that I should not feel embarrassed about the amazing siblings I have. I have encountered people who simply love because of what is on the inside.

In my opinion, the greatest gift I have ever received is unconditional love and acceptance from people who look at my siblings and see them more no different than anyone else in our world. We all are in this world together, and finding the people who do not make you feel embarrassed by your unique situation may be hard, and you may struggle, but if you put your heart and mind to it; I guarantee you that you will find people who view you for who you are and nothing else.

Steve Jobs lived life to the fullest. He had a time limit on his life like everybody else, but he did not let it stop him when he knew that it may be cut short. He exemplifies through his quote that, "Life is short, and we must focus on the people and things that make us happy. By doing so, we can overshadow the fear of concern or embarrassment. The ones who accept and love are the only ones who are important."

Growing up, I encountered many people who would not look at me for who I was because of my siblings. For whatever reason, I was different because of who my siblings were. Having siblings with special needs poses many difficulties because we are a small, select, group of people; most of our friends are not in the same boat as us and are unable to understand our trials and tribulations. When people whom have disabilities do unique things, look a distinct way, and stand out from the typical community; siblings simply feel embarrassed. It is not that they do not love their siblings for who they are, but it is rather that in our competitive world, anything less than perfect often times creates a feeling of discomfort for many people.

I encountered many different situations where I felt embarrassed. From losing friends to hiding girlfriends; I have felt embarrassed about my siblings. I regret deeply having these feelings, but I do not know how I could have changed them. There were times when my siblings did funny things in public which were embarrassing because of how people looked at us, but after understanding the needs of my siblings, I learned to just laugh at it, because we are all just living this life together. My siblings are some of the greatest people I know, and although I may be embarrassed at times, they are both perfect just the way they are. It can be hard to understand, and it will definitely take time, but feeling embarrassed will disappear if people learn to accept one another for who they are.

8

I am all alone

"Not until we are lost do we begin to understand ourselves."
-Henry David Thoreau

"Hello class! How was your weekend?"

I sat contently listening to the responses, when all of a sudden the teacher asked me to share. "So Michael, what did you do?"

I froze. Do I tell the truth? Or do I make up a story so that I fit in? I was puzzled. At no other time had I been more confused on what to say, and if you know me; you know I love to talk so this was serious.

"Well, it was ok. My sister had a Baclofen pump put in on Friday to help her with her muscle control and discomfort. After the surgery, she came home to rest and heal. A few hours later, her body exploded in hives from head to toe, and she spiked a dangerously high fever. My parents immediately rushed her back to Stanford Medical Center. She was treated by numerous doctors and nurses, and after multiple tests and evaluations, it was determined that she was having an allergic reaction to the codeine which they had given her for her pain.

They immediately changed her medications and flushed her body with fluids, and now she is back home resting." (I did not mention that it was my 13th birthday and I was hoping to enjoy a relaxing weekend with my family and friends.) My aunt was visiting from Virginia, and we were all scheduled to have dinner at the House of Genji in San Jose.)

After explaining my weekend, I immediately asked my teacher if I could use the restroom. I did not really have to go, but I did not want my classmates to see me crying. I could not hold back the tears anymore; I was vulnerable and sad. This was one of my most pivotal times in my life when I felt all alone.

No one in my class could relate to the story I had just shared. No one in my class could say that they understood half of what I just said. No one in my class could sympathize with my pain. Realistically, no one in my class probably even cared. I had just opened my life to the class, and as always, was left in isolation, knowing that I was the only one in my situation. It was just another day; another dramatic event, another day left unmatched by my peers. No encouragement to seek out others in my shoes, full of unanswered questions penetrating my brain. This was how I felt many days while growing up with my siblings. I was in a state of loneliness; a state of feeling like I was the only one in my shoes.

Growing up, I often felt alone. The only kid with siblings with special needs, the only kid who experienced all of the pain and discomfort of seeing his or her siblings live life with limitations and life threatening events. Every time that I encountered a dramatic scene, I figured that no one else had ever experienced anything similar to that of what I have, so I was left in a situation where I could not open up to anyone. I was stuck in a situation of silence. I was stuck feeling all alone.

I encountered numerous situations similar to this one. Actually, along with all of the times where I felt embarrassed; I too also felt alone in those same situations. In the many encounters I had where my siblings made me embarrassed, or when others made me feel inferior because of my siblings; I felt all alone.

There was a day during elementary school that some friends and I, along with our parents and siblings, went to California's Great America amusement park. The park, located in Santa Clara, California, is full of rides, shows and games where people from all around the Bay Area come to visit and have a good time. The day we were there was full of excitement. I was tall enough for all of the rides, and old enough to have a little freedom.

About half way through the day, my mom and sister met up with my friends and me. Because Katie was unable to go on many of the rides, my mom spent much of the day watching shows and playing games which were handicapped accessible. When we met, though, we got in line for a ride which we all could go on. The SpongeBob

Ride! A mix of a 3-D video and seats that make you feel like you are in the show. The ride is accessible for everybody.

When we got in line and grabbed our 3-D glasses, we fell in place behind some young kids. While waiting to go inside, one of the boys asked me, "Why are you waiting in line with that retard?" My heart sunk. I couldn't answer the kid, nor could I defend my sister. All I could do was sit in pure silence. The question the boy asked was out of pure ignorance, arrogance and maybe hatred; nonetheless, it set me back in my position. I was standing by my own sister, whom I love dearly, and was stuck listening to words from a boy who had no appreciation for life and the differences of all of the people in our world. The rude remarks made me feel like I was alone again. This boy, who was probably within three years of my own age, had no respect or appreciation for my sister. I don't know if he knew that we were related, but regardless, his words were cruel and unjust. I was too shy and embarrassed to stand up for her, and my silence and inferiority made me feel very isolated.

Experiencing situations where degrading comments and questions are made about disabled children can make their siblings feel alone and sad. I attended many different events where my own siblings were degraded and marginalized, but at the same time; I too, felt degraded and thus went into a state of isolation and loneliness. I could not fathom how no one else in the world could view my siblings than anything less than the perfectly imperfect persons they were. I fell into a desolate place because I was convinced nobody else in the world understood what I was going through. I felt secluded from the world because people could not view my siblings like others, and thus they could not view me as the person I was.

Growing up, I played every sport imaginable. From baseball, basketball, soccer, football, and golf; I jumped at every opportunity to engage in physical activity. It was a therapeutic place, and I loved competing with my friends. My eagerness to play ball often times carried over to my house. I wanted to play sports with my siblings. Because of my sister's disabilities, she was obviously not the one to play against. (Let me tell you, though; Katie was at darn near every one of my games, and she always was one of my biggest fans.)

So when I wanted to play at home, I had to try and get my brother, Robert, to play with me. For many years, he was much older than I, so it worked out. But as I got older, I became too strong to play with him. I would throw the ball too hard, run too fast, or be too aggressive. This led to my brother not wanting to play anymore. All I wanted to do was play with my siblings, but once again, I was alone.

I often times longed to engage in activities with my siblings. I wanted to fight, run in the park together, and do any other normal thing siblings do. I just wanted to have a strong bond. I watched as my friends interacted with their siblings, and I aspired to have similar relationships.

Not being able to interact like normal siblings left me, again, in a state of isolation. When I was home with my siblings, I did not have a friend to go rough house with or do spontaneous things. I was alone in the respect that I just did not have that special someone to go have fun with.

As a young boy, I struggled with how I could introduce friends to my siblings. Would they still be my friend if they knew my two siblings had special needs? I was scared, shy, and simply confused of how people would react, so I naturally built a wall to shield myself from the truth. I did not like to bring many friends over to my house, even though my mom often encouraged me to have friends over. Nor did I jump at the opportunity to make new friends. I was content with the friends I had, who knew my siblings already and simply looked past the idea of opening my friendship circle.

This harsh reality exists for all siblings of children with disabilities. The fear of rejection weighs a great burden on one's shoulder when trying to meet new people. Having siblings with special needs did not make this any easier. I felt alone. I built a wall around myself, and did not give others the opportunity to come in. I consequently trapped myself in a situation where I could not spread my wings and meet new people.

This attitude and fear carried over to friends of the opposite sex as well. There comes a time in your life when you get the urge to start experiencing with dating. Everybody has it. So when my time came, I once again went at a typical life stage from a different angle. Introducing girls to my family and opening my life to a potential significant other seemed like no easy task. I was afraid of rejection, I was afraid of scaring away a girl. At times, I thought that I'd just never find someone who would be comfortable with my siblings. I felt a fear that I'd be alone because of the situation I was in.

From this fear, I built a big self-inflicted barrier because I was simply afraid. I didn't know how girls would respond, so I thought that the best way to avoid heartbreak was to just not get girls involved in the first place. That was a very difficult choice; as a teenage boy, I was ready to start dating and enjoying friendships with girls. The fear of the unknown of how the girls would react to my siblings left me isolated and alone, so I simply just avoided the confrontation and decided to not bring girls into my home. I did not want the pain of a girl rejecting me because of my siblings.

Siblings of children with disabilities are left with very difficult choices. They experience feelings which nobody else does. They have to make choices which some people never even dream about, and they usually have to do it on big, important issues. Growing up with my siblings, I did not know how to introduce friends of either sex to my family. I wanted to expand my friendship circle, but the fear of rejection left me content with what I had and already trusted. The circumstances were rough, and from it all, I was left in a state of loneliness.

While trying to accept my life and the life of my siblings, I felt isolated. I believed that I was the only person who had to experience my life's conditions, and I felt that even when I was surrounded by my siblings, I was alone. I just could not grasp the different lifestyle.

Siblings of children with disabilities face many emotions unique to themselves. They feel alone at times because they almost never see young kids living similar lives to theirs. They look at their classmates and usually do not know of another kid who has a sibling with special needs. This leads to isolation because they just feel like nobody understands what they are going through. Although they may be right some of the time, it is important to not be afraid to open your life to others and give them the opportunity to see life from your eyes. Similarly, they are frequently left in situations where they do not receive the same attention as their siblings. These occurrences lead to a state of feeling alone. They understand that they are loved and admired by their family and loved ones, but at the same time their special conditions inevitably lead to feelings of isolation. Growing up, I felt lonely, and I longed for closure to help me move forward with the life I was supposed to have.

9

Finding His Footprints

"The moment you stop accepting challenges
is the moment you stop moving forward."
-Unknown

*T*think when tragedy or hardship occurs in our lives, we are
presented a choice. We can either give in to the emptiness,
the anger, and the fear trying to ruin our lives, or we can try to find
the meaning behind it all. Over the course of my life thus far, I have
spent many days confused, jealous, embarrassed, and even alone.

These immense feelings were not going to make me a better person nor help me live a life full of richness and love. Instead, these feelings were damaging the life I had. They were simply there holding me back and restricting me from spreading my wings and fostering my own life.

I knew early on in my life that my siblings were different. I knew early on that I lived a different life than most of the world, at the same time; I thought that my different life was some kind of a bad thing. I determined that the harsh negative comments that were made by friends and strangers alike were conclusive to the fact that my life was uniquely different. I felt that nobody could accept this life, not even myself.

Having two siblings with special needs is unique. There are not many people in this world who can say that they live in this situation, but this occurrence was something that I had no control over. From infancy, I was placed in a life where I was the younger sibling to two siblings with special needs. It was something I had to accept, and not look back.

While trying to accept my life and the life of my siblings, I felt isolated. I felt that I was the only kid who had to experience my condition. I remember one day in school, when a kid came into class and started talking about how he was so mad with his younger sister because she had put a Barbie in his backpack. He was furious, but he felt that the other kids in the class could sympathize for him because they too had a sister or brother whom bothered them.

This made me think. Could I come into class and start a conversation and relate to other kids? If I said that last night I was in the hospital until eleven p.m. with my sister because she was having an allergic reaction to a medication that she had after she had a Baclofen pump operation. Would anybody relate? No, they would not. I was isolated because others could not relate to me. They did not know half of the things I knew from growing up with siblings with special needs, and thus I had nobody to reach out to and talk with. I felt alone.

Along with isolation came embarrassment. I was embarrassed by my siblings multiple times. As sad as it sounds, I wished that I could have sometimes been isolated away from my siblings so that I would not have to associate with them because I was just simply embarrassed. I was not embarrassed because I did not love them; I was embarrassed because young ignorant kids could not get past the fact that I was a normal kid despite having siblings with special needs. I was looked at differently, and I was embarrassed by what I was judged upon.

I remember a time when I was performing in a winter concert for my junior high band. We had just finished playing our opening piece, and we were about to start *Silent Night*. The whole auditorium quieted, and the lights were dimmed. A sense of Christmas cheer filled the air. As the violins started playing, out came a big screech of excitement. I knew exactly who it was. Katie recognized the song, and out of a love for Christmas, she screeched in joy. I was embarrassed. The entire audience turned to my sister as she disrupted the show. People then started looking at me because they knew that she was my sister. All I could do was just shrug my shoulders. When you look at the big picture, it wasn't necessarily bad that she screeched, but nonetheless it was embarrassing because it was at a time when everyone else was silent.

Through these challenges, I needed more than ever to find a way to accept the life I had been given and find the reasoning behind it all. I began back on the trail of finding my answer. I again talked and read, and then I came across two quotes that helped me understand how to accept life's challenges.

All throughout growing up, my parents told me that there was a reason I was selected to grow up with two siblings, and that someday I would be able to realize it. I tried to believe that, but it was difficult when constant disappointments occurred. After reading this quote, I was able to believe my parents' words. I was able to grasp the idea that someday I would find the blessings of my siblings. Katie and Robert may, from the outside, be an immense trial in my life. Their extra needs and difficult lifestyles pose many complicated situations to my family; but the quote allowed me to look further. Was there a blessing in my sibling's unique lives? Do they provide me something that I cannot find anywhere else? I came to believe that they did, and that helped me accept their disabilities.

Katie and Robert are the most loving, supportive, people I have ever met; and they bring me an immense amount of joy. Despite their obvious setbacks, they provide me so much love in my life. After I could accept the fact that there was going to be a blessing in disguise someday; I was able to continue on with my journey. I was able to feel confident in my shoes, and I was able to feel welcomed in a world not familiar with my own. Understanding that I was going to receive a blessing that nobody else was going to receive was all that I needed to keep my life moving ahead.

It was the summer of 2015, and I was staying at the beach house for our week long stay every summer with all of my aunts and cousins. Sadly, that year, as you will learn more about later; Katie was extremely sick and in the hospital, so she never was able to come over and stay with us. Despite the obvious sorrow, it still was a very memorable time with my brother and all of my cousins.

On Wednesday, I awoke to a cold, foggy morning. It was about 50 degrees out with no blue sky overhead. I awoke, said good morning to my cousins, and ate breakfast. After breakfast however; I was just not feeling right. I needed to do something more to find some happiness. I decided I wanted to grab my Bible and go for a walk on the beach to find some solace with the Lord.

I got a ways down the beach and opened up to a random page in my Bible. I knew the Lord would find a way to put me in a passage that would bring comfort and healing to me. Man, did He provide. The passage I turned to was none other than chapter 9 of the book of John.

I began to read: "As he went along, he saw a man blind from birth. His disciples asked Him, 'Rabbi, who sinned, this man or his parents, that he was born blind?' 'Neither this man nor his parents sinned,' said Jesus, 'but this happened so that the works of God might be displayed in him. As long as it is day, we must do the works of him who sent me. Night is coming, when no one can work. While I am in the world, I am the light of the world.'" (John 9: 1-5 NIV)

This passage immediately made me freeze in my thoughts, and divulged more into what God was trying to tell me. All throughout the challenges I have faced, I have been in question as to why all of this hardship has occurred, but right there and then; God showed me he was in control and that I must follow his lead in my life. I knew growing up that Katie and Robert were not disabled based on a mistake they had made. For one, Robert was diagnosed with his disabilities at birth. There was no possible way for him to sin and be reprimanded for his actions.

Similarly, Katie was an honest loving girl, whom only broke a rule when she took two cookies out of the cookie jar when she had been instructed to take one. I know that we have all done that before, and have not been afflicted with disabilities, so she was not being punished. But the message Jesus shares is that each and every person is created for a reason. Katie and Robert were created to share something special. They were picked by God to share His love. God's divine intervention intercepted my life. His footprints were revealed.

Understanding that God had personally chosen my siblings to show His love was a way for me to accept my siblings' disabilities. It was a way for me to cherish my siblings and know that they were placed on this planet for a distinct purpose. As I was able to accept why my siblings were disabled; I was also able to accept as to why I was chosen to have two siblings with special needs. Understanding that God chooses people to show His love is all I needed to know. I was able to realize that the lessons I learn from the trying circumstances I have undergone will be passed on to the rest of the world through me. I was content knowing that I was to be a messenger of God. Hearing God's words in the Bible was an essential part of accepting my siblings' disabilities, but it was absolutely necessary.

I remember going on a retreat in high school and coming across the story of *Jesus' Footprints in the Sand*. As you may already know, the story goes that a man was walking with Jesus on the beach when a devastating storm hit. The storm was rough and tough and battered the man. When it hit, he saw only one pair of footprints in the sand. He asked Jesus, "Why, when I have needed you the most, have you not been there for me?" Jesus responded in his delightful way and said, "The times when you have seen only one set of footprints is when I carried you."

I have undergone many stormy days in my life. There were nights I went to bed alone as my parents were in the hospital with Katie, and there were nights I simply could not sleep because I worried for my two siblings and how the future was going to treat them. I was scared and overcome by emotion. I thought I was alone, too, at times on the sand walking by myself, without anybody there by my side. I believed I was walking through my life alone. I was wrong. God was with me and my siblings through it all.

When Katie was sick in the hospital, He was beside her. When Robert is volunteering for so many different teams, he is showing God's love and God is with him. When I am laying in bed worrying about my future with my siblings, God is lying beside me. God is with us through every trial we face, and He certainly was not leaving me alone to handle the situation I had.

Coming to terms with a confusing situation is a light that can ignite a new future. After accepting the fact that I was going to live with two siblings with special needs; my heart switched from needing sympathy, to giving sympathy to others. I was able to digest the fact that I was going to lead a different life, but it was a life that I was more than capable of living. I liked to think growing up, that despite traveling a different path in life than that of my peers, in the end, we would all return to the same destination. This belief allowed me to fully embrace my life and go at it like I would go at any life. I was assured that I would get to the same place in the end, but I would just have to travel a different road.

An example of this was going to see a Giants baseball game. Both disabled people and non-disabled people can go to the game, but the way it is done is different. For example, my family would drive to the game, and we would buy tickets in the handicapped section. We would go a little early to see batting practice, and we would stay until the final pitch was thrown. On the other hand, a non-disabled family might go to the game on the train, get tickets directly on the third-base line, and also arrive early to see some of batting practice.

You see, we took very different routes to the game, but in the end, we both watched the same game. Living life follows this same mentality. Growing up with siblings with special needs taught me the fact that although we may do things differently, we are still able to do the same things as everyone else. We will definitely take a different route, but in the end we will be at the same destination.

Each of our lives are dealt different hands of cards. Some people are dealt the best cards, and some are dealt the worst, but no matter what cards are received, each person can play the game. Our lives are all different. Some people face immense struggles, some people face minimal struggles. Do not mistake me, because each life has its share of difficulties; our faith and love is tried multiple times. There are times when we are stretched to our limits and we feel that there is no hope for a future, but through these trying times, a greater destination is going to prevail. When we can accept a situation as it arises, and fully engage ourselves in the future, we can make any situation a success. Each and every difficult time teaches us something if we open our hearts and eyes to it. We are always given something we can handle, and there is always a lesson we will learn.

Growing up with two siblings with special needs was hard. I was stretched to my limits multiple times, but I was able to accept that I did not have a choice, and I was inspired to live my life with the hope of creating a future where I am able to share the blessings that my siblings have provided. Accepting my unique life allowed me to find the hope and courage I needed to conquer this life. I was able to love life like I never had loved it before. Accepting why I lived this life was the light I needed for my life to continue.

Tragedy surrounds us. From disease, freak accidents, and other unfortunate events, every one faces situations which are hard to comprehend. Through these tough times though, it is important to accept the situation as it is, and find the reason and meaning behind it all. For me, finding God's footprints in my life was how I overcame the initial struggles of growing up with siblings with special needs. There were days that I felt all alone, and there were days that I just could not fathom why I had to live the life I did, but by finding God's grace I found a newfound hope for my future ahead and saw myself leading a life that God wanted me to lead.

I think when tragedy or hardship occurs in our lives, we are presented a choice. We can either give in to the emptiness, anger, or fear trying to ruin our lives, or we can try to find the meaning behind it, grasp the challenge, conquer it, and focus on the hope that exists in everything around us with God by our side. Over the course of my life thus far, I have spent many days confused, jealous, embarrassed, and even lonely at times trying to understand the life I have been given. Those feelings were not going to make me a better person, nor aid me in living a life full of solace and love. Instead, those feelings were damaging the life I had. They were simply there, holding me back and restricting me from spreading my wings and fostering my own life.

How do you overcome struggles when they seem never-ending with little reasoning? How do you move forward with love and courage when life seems unfair? These were thoughts that kept me from foraging ahead. They restricted me from taking life head on, and I needed to find a new strength to move forward, but what strength would that be? Where could I find the power to take on life's uncertainly?

Well, in my case; God. God is what I needed to find in order to accept my situation and propel forward. Finding His footprints and knowing that He was in control of my life and my siblings' was the knowledge I needed to heal and overcome. I needed to find His footprints in my life and locate the reason my life was unfolding the way that it was. By finding God's footprints in my life, I was at a newfound place knowing that everything was going to good and that there was a greater reasoning behind it all for myself and for Katie and Robert. God is displayed in every situation and ever tribulation people have to overcome. Finding His footprints gave me a new way to go about my life, and I have since never looked back.

Life has a way of throwing curveballs at us when we least expect it or deserve it. By the grace of God and faith in Christ; we all can conquer the highest mountain and the longest mile alike. Knowing Christ in times of difficulty will not only give us comfort when we need it most, but it will strengthen our love for one another and God Himself. We may be dealt a bad hand, but we are never dealt a hand that we cannot win with. God's hand is always open and ready for our grasp. Finding God's footprints will give you the strength to move forward, and it will give you comfort knowing that there is a Savior on your team for the highs and lows of life. Find God's footprints in your life, and grasp His love as you overcome your life's struggles.

We will triumph, and we will fail, but throughout all of our journeys, Christ will carry us though. He will always walk with us. As Joshua 1:9 reads in the NIV, "This is my command. Be strong and courageous. Do not be afraid or discouraged. For the Lord your God is with you wherever you go."

10

Angels are Everywhere

"God allows us to experience the low points of life in order to teach us lessons we could learn no other way."
- C.S Lewis

One of the earliest appearances of Jesus after the crucifixion and revelation of the empty tomb and His resurrection was on the Road to Emmaus. Cleopas, a disciple, as well as one other disciple were on the road to Emmaus headed for supper. While walking on the road, a man was revealed next to them. The man, as we later learned, was Jesus. The two disciples did not recognize Jesus though, as He was walking by their side, and they did not engage with the man as they would have if they had known who he was.

The disciples and the man talked for a little while, and they convinced the man to join them for supper. Jesus graciously accepted the offer and went with the disciples. When they all gathered to eat, the men suddenly realized who the man was. Different revelations made them come to learn that they were indeed in the presence of the Lord. Although, when the disciples recognized Jesus; He immediately disappeared. Jesus was not recognized by the two disciples when He was walking by their side, but when He was recognized at supper He vanished from sight. The Gospel of John reads, "Were not our hearts burning within us while he talked with us on the road and opened the Scriptures to us?" (John 24:32 NIV)

One of the hardest things about having faith is the fact that Jesus figuratively cannot be seen walking beside us. One cannot reach out a hand and touch Jesus, but, Jesus does in fact walk beside us, and his love and affection for us is revealed in many ways. Having siblings with special needs makes it hard at times to see Jesus. It is impossible to see His body, so having faith in Him is even harder to fathom. However, when I found Jesus' footprints, I also found revelations of Jesus' body in my and my siblings' lives. He was revealed to my eye.

People with special needs live a very unique and challenging life. Many people simply do not know how to respond to the various needs of the individual and understand their challenges. Many friends may abandon you as they simply believe that it is the best way to cope with the situation due to their lack of understanding and empathy. Despite the friends that turn away, others come forward and rise above and offer you more love and support than ever before. People selflessly give themselves to you and do everything in their power to help you overcome the challenges that you face. These people are angels.

Many different people in my life have been revealed to be angels to me. Their love and compassion is endless, and they provide more than I ever could have imagined. Their love for my siblings and me is incomparable, and the impacts they have made are endless. They have been Jesus walking beside us. They have shown Christ's love.

When angels give themselves to others, you can see the love and joy exuberating out of their body. Angels love and give unconditionally. They never do it for fame or recognition. Despite that, I think that it is only fair to show the world how angels in my life have affected me and my siblings, and how they have showed me Jesus walking beside us. The people you will hear about did not do what they did because they knew I was going to write a book, nor did they do it to make a personal benefit; they simply acted selflessly to benefit my siblings and my life. That, to me, is an act of an angel. By finding God's footprints, I was able to see Jesus acting through others to display his unconditional love, and the people I have encountered have made everlasting impacts on my life.

It all begins with a man who my family does not even know. A man who donated his bone marrow to Katie for a bone marrow transplant in hopes of giving her a second chance on life. Katie's bone marrow donor requested anonymity when deciding that it was in his wish to donate bone marrow. The donor knew he was a 4 out of 5 match for Katie and was willing to go through the hours of tests and preparation for the bone marrow draw. Despite this, the selfless donor went through the very painful procedure to be able to help save Katie's life.

Jesus was certainly walking beside us at this time. Why would a random man decide to give bone marrow to someone he did not know? To this day, the donor still does not know how Katie is doing. After a year post transplant, my parents requested that if he would like to meet with our family, they would love to thank him and tell him what a success the bone marrow transplant had been. He was not interested in identifying himself, but he did send a nice card wishing Katie well. So, when people say that it is impossible to see Jesus walking with you; I disagree. This donor was how Jesus saved Katie. The man's decision to donate his bone marrow was a very courageous and selfless act, and as one looks back to see how Jesus could be revealed in such a difficult situation, this man is the evidence of Christ by your side.

Every year, thousands of people donate blood, bone marrow, and organs with hope that their sacrifices could benefit the life of another human being. From heart transplants to bone marrow transplants, there are endless situations where people will benefit from the sacrifices of others. People who donate blood or organs give the ultimate gift of life and giving love and hope to so many people. Many people are living today because of organ donations by the angels in our lives. It is clear to me that the man who donated his bone marrow to Katie was one of Jesus' angels here on earth.

Because of the care that Katie requires at home when she is not at school, caregivers became an important part of my family as I was growing up. When I was in the third grade, my mother was a stay at home mom for many years before returning back to work as a teacher. When she began teaching, it became clear that more help was going to be needed around the house to help care for Katie. With this need we found the perfect answer, a lady I learned to consider as a second mom for so long.

Originally from Ethiopia, Haiba was an angel from God who came into our life at the perfect time. Haiba was an aide at Katie's school for many years, but when my family decided to reach out for help, she excitedly came to be a caregiver for Katie and a second mom to me. Haiba could do it all. She would take Katie to the movies, the mall, and out to lunch. She would always take care of Katie at home by feeding her, changing her, and she loved to bathe Katie. Whenever extra help was needed, Haiba was there in a heartbeat.

Haiba loved Katie as if she were her own, and did everything in her power for ten years to give Katie the love, care, and support she deserved. Haiba's love for our family was immense, and her determination and work ethic was unmatched. She was Jesus walking beside as she aided us whenever we needed, and provided endless love and support. She is definitely an angel to who we could never fully repay. She was invited to family functions and became one of my mother's best friends. Despite living in Georgia now, Haiba's profound love and devotion had an everlasting impact on my family and it will never be forgotten. Her angelic deeds for our family will never be replaced.

After Haiba relocated to Georgia, into our life came another angel. TJ, also from Ethiopia, immediately filled the void of Haiba and took off right where Haiba left off. TJ is the ultimate caregiver who loves Katie dearly, and always strives to give Katie her all. She meets Katie at our house almost every day after school, and stays with her all afternoon until my mom or dad gets back from work. She feeds Katie and takes care of her, and even on special occasions accompanies her to the mall or movies as well. She is an angel, as her primary goal is to make Katie feel loved and valued. She works endlessly to give Katie all that she needs and a little more. TJ's selfless lifestyle is that of an angel as she does it all for the purpose of others and not for herself.

People with disabilities require extra care. Their special needs make it difficult for parents to provide for them as well as do what else has to be done in their lives and in their homes. Into these voids come caregivers who act as the epitome of Christ. Caregivers do not do their work for personal gain, nor do they do their work to be recognized by others. They simply feel the desire to give themselves to others and provide for people when they cannot provide for themselves.

Growing up with my two siblings exposed me to these amazing people whom my family considers angels. We have greatly benefited from the acts and hard work of these individuals, as well as seen how many other families have benefited as well. There is nothing more heartwarming to me than to see somebody graciously devote themselves to my sister and help her do anything that she wants to do.

The servant spirit of the caregivers is to be admired by all, and they deserve all the praise in the world as their work is nothing short of angelic. Caregivers of people with special needs are angels on this earth, and deserve to know how much they mean to families.

My brother Robert was in high school attending Branham High School when he met the man I aspired to be. Robert met Josh Lagod through the Best Buddies program at his high school. Best Buddies pairs a general education high school student with a student in the special education department and the students meet on a regular basis. There is even a Best Buddies Prom. The program is run through the school, but from the moment Robert met Josh, it was something that simply went above and beyond the traditional program.

The first time we met Josh was when he drove to our house to pick Robert up before the two were to go to a Stanford football game. My grandfather, at the time, was a season ticket holder. Because it was a cold, rainy day, my grandfather was uninterested in going to the game. My grandfather asked Robert to invite a friend. Robert quickly jumped at the opportunity and invited Josh to join him. Josh graciously accepted the offer and jumped at the opportunity to come pick Robert up and drive up to Stanford for the game.

From the moment we first met Josh, we knew he was an angel for Robert. The two became instant friends. Josh was on the football and basketball team at the school, and Robert was a team manager. They were always together at games, and Josh would invite Robert to hang out with the team after the games. He engaged Robert like no other, and helped Robert develop a huge friend group. Josh's selfless actions towards Robert were unparalleled, and the impact he made on Robert's life was endless. Even today, twelve years later, the two frequently get together and go out to dinner, attend a game, or socialize on birthdays. Josh is simply an amazing person.

Despite Josh being assigned as a buddy to Robert, he went above that call and became a family friend to our entire family. One person he took a quick liking to though, was Katie. Katie absolutely adores Josh, and he absolutely adores Katie. For the past twelve years the two have been inseparable whenever Josh is around. He holds Katie's hand and gives her a kiss on the cheek whenever he sees her, and he always treats her like a princess. He looks past her special needs and loves her for the girl that she is. He has attended all of her birthday parties over the years and has been her poster boy. Josh's selfless love towards Katie and Robert has made him an angel to our family. He is the person I will always aspire to be. Josh, too, is an angel in our life.

In our life we have come across so many family and friends who have been so special to us. People have brought dinners for us when Katie was staying in hospital, and people even helped take care of me when I was a young child in need of a little extra care when my parents were busy elsewhere. All of this help was noticed, and appreciated more than the people will ever know. One friend of my mom has constantly been at our side throughout the entire journey. Her name is Pam Berry. Pam met my mom when her son, Matthew and Robert were in Cub Scouts together. The two boys became friends, and my mom and Pam became very good friends as well. When we went away to Minnesota for Katie's Bone Marrow Transplant; Pam constantly kept in contact with us and gave us support from far away. Her love was endless. Pam even came to Minnesota to offer her support and take Robert with her to travel around Wisconsin, where her family is from.

Over the years, Pam has continuously been a soldier for our family, assisting us whenever we need it. Just last summer, when Katie spent almost two weeks in the hospital, Pam's amazing support was exemplified the most. After Katie failed a swallow study and was unable to eat solid food, her diet quickly changed. Katie was protein deficient from the new puree diet, and needed a protein supplement. Pam went to the store for my mom to get Katie some protein shakes to help her get enough protein to fight off the illness she was battling.

When she came back to the hospital, she also brought a very nice picnic dinner for my family to eat. The homemade fresh food tasted so good after eating hospital food for a week. Pam simply went above and beyond to make sure my parents knew that she was on their team for the fight. Pam is definitely an angel to our family, as her love for us is seen so many ways as she always offers a helping hand when we need it the most. Pam is also the definition of Jesus walking beside us, and shows us all how we can see angels everywhere we look.

The final individual I want to single out is a man who I know will definitely be sitting on the right hand of God in Heaven. Nick Palermo, the man who wrote the foreword to this book, is a man who has made the world a much better place.

People always ask what is the greatest accomplishment one can do while here on earth. For people into space, it may be to walk on the moon, like Neil Armstrong. For people into green technology, it may be creating an all electric car, like Elon Musk. However, when you ask me, the greatest accomplishment I can think of would be to always leave an impact on the people I encounter and to leave the world a better place than how I found it, like what Nick Palermo did with Young Life Capernaum thirty years ago.

In 1986, Nick Palermo held his first Young Life Club in San Jose for students with disabilities, and now 30 years later there are clubs like those held all around the world. A club that started in San Jose is now an international phenomenon because of Nick Palermo, and the world certainly is a better place because of the vision he had, and the avenue for which he created for thousands of lives to be touched by Christ.

Young Life Capernaum is a ministry that focuses on touching the lives of people with special needs. From weekly clubs, dances, and summer camp; Young Life Capernaum leaves everlasting impacts on all of the lives it touches. Nick Palermo started the ministry when he saw kids with special needs constantly having nothing to do. He was alarmed that they never had a place to hangout, so he saw a vision of creating a sacred place for them to have fun while experiencing the love of Christ. He created a weekly club for everyone to have fun. His heart for others is incomparable, and his passion for creating a life full of love for all of God's children is unbeatable.

Katie has been attending Young Life Capernaum since she was in high school. She started attending the weekly club meetings, and then slowly integrated into attending all of the events which took place. From day camp in San Jose, to summer camp at Lost Canyon

Young Life Camp in Arizona; Katie has directly benefited from the ministry that Nick created. Further, I have been a volunteer for the ministry for years, and have first handedly seen what a profound impact Nick has made on the special needs community. His actions will never be replaced as he gave a new life to so many kids left without something to do.

Nick has had a profound impact on my life. I have learned from Nick that by having a vision of love and meaning, the world can be a better place for all. Nick is the epitome of an angel of God as he pursued his love of God by helping the marginalized and creating a place for them to be loved. His passion for Christ and sharing The Word to people with special needs is something I will always hold dear to my heart. Nick has acted as Jesus on this planet, but more importantly has been an angel to our family. Every parent fears about what the life of their child with special needs will be like. With Nick, and the Capernaum ministry, he has inspired many people to do Gods work. I do not think any parent has to fear anymore. Thank you Nick, for hearing your calling and making this world a better place for people with disabilities.

Despite being able to write a whole book just on the amazing individuals my family and I have encountered and who have revealed Jesus walking with us; I want to transition to two groups of people who display Christ's love to us all: medical professionals and special education personnel. Medical professionals, ranging from neurologists to speech therapists, devote their lives to helping others. They are the direct hands of God doing work on this planet to help all who need it. Over the course of growing up, I have seen Katie and Robert both benefit from medical professionals who graciously give their services to better humanity. I have seen physical therapists strap Katie onto a bike and help Katie ride it and help her feel free. Neurosurgeons have given Robert a second chance on life. The medical professionals are the hands of God doing His work on this planet. They are angels on this planet as their love and service towards my siblings are unmatched, and are due an immense amount of praise. They are truly amazing people, and every one of them should be loved and respected for the decision they made to spend their lives assisting others.

In addition to medical professionals, special education teachers and aides are people who deserve recognition for the careers they have chosen to help some of the most vulnerable in our society. Special education teachers and aides make dramatic impacts on the lives of children with special needs . Katie and Robert have always loved to ride the bus to school and participate in school to the fullest. They have enjoyed their experiences because of those who are involved: the teachers and the paraprofessionals.

Teachers who choose to go into special education are a rare breed, as their classrooms will never be like that of their counterparts. They do not teach by any traditional means, but they will impact the lives of all of their students in unimaginable ways. Paraprofessionals who assist kids with special needs are angels in their own right as they give up their own time to make students with disabilities get the most out of their time at school. Their drive to assist the teachers in the classroom is beautiful to see as they create a place where the students can have an enjoyable place to go.

For some kids with special needs, their only outing is to school, and so the impact and setting teachers and paraprofessionals create is so important for the development of these students and it is appreciated greatly. Seeing Katie and Robert's teachers and paraprofessionals at work, providing a caring a nurturing environment, is priceless. Jesus was the ultimate teacher, but special education teachers and paraprofessional are angels on this planet as they give themselves to the life of kids with special needs on a daily basis. Looking at all they do makes it impossible not to see Jesus on this journey with us.

Finally, random people whom we have encountered throughout our lives have been deemed angels on this planet. Over the course of growing up, I have seen countless people do amazing things for no good reason but to just show some love to my siblings. For one, Robert is involved highly with many sports teams in the area. He has been a team manager at both the high school and college level, fulfilling his passion and finding a brotherhood of his own. All of these teams have had players and coaches come forward showing God's love to Robert.

In high school, Robert helped the football, basketball, and baseball teams for four years. He would go to their practices, games, and team gatherings. He was a part of the team and he loved it! After the conclusion of his four years at the school, the athletic department named an award after Robert, "The Robbie Deauville Award." This award was named after Robert for his passion for the athletic department, and to this day, is still awarded to two graduating seniors.

Robert was touched immensely by so many people in the athletes department at Branham, and their love for him was reciprocated. Branham was amazing to Robert. Many different coaches and players have also given so much to Robert, and their love for him shows me that angels are everywhere we look and, again, shows us Jesus walking beside us.

Similarly, many strangers have shown completely random acts of kindness for Katie over the years. One day at Nordstrom's, one of the makeup specialists volunteered to do Katie's makeup for free. The young lady, no older than thirty, had worked with a child with special needs before, and thus was inspired to give back. Her heart of gold was so clear to my family when we saw this event occur, and she acted so selflessly to Katie and gave her a makeover she will never forget. We experienced this girl's selfless nature, and once again, a random person in our community noticed my siblings' difficulties and tried to give them a little extra love where she could.

A similar occurrence occurred at Universal Studios one spring when my mom, my sister, and I accompanied my aunt and her family to enjoy a weekend at the theme park. We were waiting for the bus to take us from the hotel to the park when a florist was carrying flowers through the hotel lobby for a wedding. Katie had her typical big smile on her face, and greeted the florist. The man, probably in his fifties, instantly lit up and gave Katie a big hello. He continued his duties into the hotel, but later came out with 2 roses.

Placing the roses on Katie's tray, he told her to have a great day. The florist was just doing his job, but saw Katie and thought to do something to brighten her day. This small, yet profound act, gave Katie a moment of happiness, but gave me tears of joy as I saw random people give my sister a little extra love and attention. He was an angel from God that morning.

Throughout my life, I have seen so many people give themselves to my siblings and show God's love to them. In Greek, "agape" is described as the love one shows to God as well as the love God shows to man. I have seen agape love from so many people in my life. I have been able to see God's hands on my siblings and my life as we have conquered our lives. Jesus cannot be seen on this earth, but people can be seen doing what Jesus would do. Thus, He can be seen. Growing up and accepting Christ as having His hands on our lives has enabled me to see Jesus walking beside us. From the angels in people we have encountered, I have been able to find God's love and know that He is in control and that He is going to place people in our lives that show us that He is in control.

The angels that Katie saw on the flight to Minnesota ought to be the angels that have permeated through our lives and made everything ok. The people I have shared with you are angels, and I know that they have been sent to us from above. Angels are everywhere, and they give us so much strength along our journey of life.

11

Smiling Through Tears

"Everybody is genius. But if you judge a fish by its ability to climb
a tree, it will live it's whole life believing that it is stupid."
- Albert Einstein

I sank down into my bed, covering myself with the warm
comforter, as I smiled from ear to ear after celebrating
my sister's twenty-first birthday at our beach house in Aptos. The
waves were crashing on the shore, and I could hear them perfectly

because my grandmother always insisted that the sliding glass door be cracked open in order to hear the water. My parents, Aunt Nancy, Aunt Carolyn, Robert, and Josh were not home yet with my sister from the Rio Del Mar bar where my sister was going to have her first sip of alcohol. I was satisfied with the idea of going to bed early with my cousins, without having to stay up and watch a movie with my uncle. I wanted to fall asleep before I heard the crowd come in and wake me up. All I wanted to do was fall asleep to the sounds of the crashing waves and occasional seagull squawks.

As sleep drifted in to close my eyes and fall fast asleep; my mind switched from in and out of conscious thought. Different thoughts and ideas were traveling around my head as fast as the sardines swimming in the ocean a few hundred yards away from where I lay. The thoughts were so immense and powerful that I had trouble remembering what was real, and what was a dream. I felt like I did not remember Katie in a wheelchair anymore.

I could not remember her diagnosis. I envisioned her running on the beach with me as we chased the pelicans and seagulls. I could not find the place in me which realized that she was in a wheelchair and could not walk or speak clearly. I forgot that she could not draw a picture of the pretty landscape we were staring at. The thoughts and realization that she was different escaped my head. Her disabilities were stuck in some part of my brain that was closed that night. My gratitude for life and love of the prior events locked up my thoughts of sadness and sympathy. Memories of playing hide and go seek played in my head, until I realized that I was just dreaming.

"Who is my sister?" was the question my dream induced brain asked. "Can she walk like me? Are my memories all wrong and mistaken? Was it a nightmare that my sister had special needs?"

Then…the familiar screech and laughter rolled around the walls of the house as my mom rolled my sister up the ramp and into the house. I jumped out of bed, and threw on some sweats. In a few seconds, my sister's wheelchair would be rolling down the hall and into the living room.

"Hi, Miiiii-chael!" Katie shouted as she saw me walk into the room. Katie had no control or idea of when she was screaming loudly, so her friendly greeting made the windows shake, and woke the house. She normally would be sound asleep by 11 p.m., but that night was an exception. My grandma asked her how her night out was on the first night of being twenty-one, and her response was, "Oh yeah, Baby!" Evidently, that was also her exact response when she had her first taste of a strawberry daiquiri.

This was not a common phrase that Katie used, so I inferred that it meant that she had a very good time. My mom informed us that she had one sip of a strawberry daiquiri, and she absolutely loved it. Then she drank the rest of a virgin margarita. (She cannot have too much alcohol because of her seizure medications.)

It is common to celebrate the milestone of turning twenty-one. For most people, the celebration is because the individual is old enough to legally consume alcohol. Despite that, this milestone of my sister turning twenty-one meant much more to my family. My sister was celebrating her fourteenth birthday following a diagnosis and bone marrow transplant which often cuts lives off far too short.

It is moments like these where I understand the hidden blessings that my siblings have been, and find the gratitude for life I have been given. It's moments like these where I smile through tears. There are so many occurrences where hardships arise in peoples' lives that cause them to shed tears. In those same lives, however, there are other amazing deeds that emerge that cause one to smile. So despite their being many tears in Katie's life from all of her challenges, there still are many times when we can all smile through those tears.

Resilience–the ability to recover quickly from difficulties.

Derived from the Latin word resili; resilience is the term coined to show one's ability to come back from difficult trials and move forward with their life. Having two siblings with special needs gave me and my family many different challenges in life that needed to be overcome. Countless times, we have been in difficult situations unsure of the ending result. As a sibling, I repeatedly saw my sibling undergo trying times at the doctor's office, school, therapy sessions, or the park. Katie and Robert constantly overcame the challenges that were posed to them and, ultimately, looked forward to a brighter tomorrow. My siblings taught me to be resilient by example. My siblings taught me to smile through tears.

Being a sibling to two children with special needs exposed me to situations where we were unable to do many normal activities. Whether it was going on a hike up the mountain; riding bikes to the store to get an ice cream, going swimming in the pool, or putting our toes in the sand. The fact that Katie was in a wheelchair made many everyday activities very challenging for the family to participate in. Many activities we participated in were not done with the ease that most people find.

Seeing that my siblings' difficulties put restrictions on what we did made me very upset at times. There were days that all I wanted to do was be in my friends' shoes and do things simply. Sadly, I could not. For example, just going swimming in the community pool required a great effort to get Katie into the pool. My mom had to lift her into the pool and then, one of her friends or I would have to hold Katie until my mom could get into the water. Getting her out of the water was also a big lift and it just seemed that everyone around the pool watched and did not help. I was often embarrassed at the extra attention drawn to the situation. I grew sad, and angry, and simply annoyed because I just wanted to do things the way my friends did. I wanted to be a normal sibling without all the extra attention and embarrassment that went along with it.

This belief did not come nor disappear overnight. I always just wanted to do something the normal way. Time after time though, it became evident that that was not going to happen. Our family still went to the beach, went swimming, went on walks, and took Katie and Robert with us. Katie could participate in many things, but often more energy and effort was required to figure out how to make the activity accessible to her. By finding God's grace and seeing Him walk the road beside us, it became clear that my siblings and I could do anything normal siblings could do, but we just had to do it our own unique way. Many times I just put on blinders and did not look at the people looking at us as we figured out ways to make activities work for Katie.

An example of smiling through tears and being resilient occurred a few summers ago. For the past ten years, my grandma has invited my mom and her sisters and families to the beach house. We would all gather at the house the first week of August and enjoy a week together soaking up the California sun. It was always a highlight of the summer.

Every year when we went to the house, Katie would be stuck on the deck with my grandmother, unable to go down to the sand.

There was a large flight of stairs between the deck and the sand, and there was no way to get Katie down the stairs without the help of at least two to three strong men. When my grandmother was alive, Katie would spend time on the deck with Grandma. The summer after Grandma passed away, it dawned on me that something else had to be done for Katie to enjoy her time there. For years, I always had felt badly that Katie could not go down to the beach and put her toes in the sand and the ocean water. I was determined to do something about it.

I drove to the local Ace Hardware store in Campbell, California and began my search for a large wagon. I walked around the store for a few minutes, and then out popped the perfect wagon. I found what I was searching for; it was big enough to hold Katie and the wheels were large enough to roll over the sand. The metal wagon was not the most comfortable to lie down in, though. So, the next week I went back to the store to purchase wood to make a backrest for Katie. After a few days of measuring, cutting, and building, the perfect wagon was built for Katie to sit up in. Wow, I was quite proud of myself.

Beach week arrived, and we packed the vans and headed to the beach. We arrived at our usual time around 3:00 p.m. and quickly settled into our beach house at Rio Del Mar. I quickly arranged pillows and towels in the wagon so Katie would be comfortable as we pulled her to the beach. My mom pushed Katie to the front of the house and transferred Katie from her wheelchair to her wagon. I then pulled Katie down the street with my cousins, past four or five houses to get her where we could enter the beach. With my cousins pushing the wagon, and me pulling the wagon; Katie was on the sand! It took a lot of strength and effort, but we finally pulled her down to the water. For the first time in fifteen years, that beautiful girl put her toes in the mighty cold Pacific Ocean. Success. Katie was on the beach.

You see, difficulties simply arrive because of the disabilities disabling people from doing simple tasks. These difficulties though, can be overcome if one is resilient and finds alternative ways to get the job done. Seeing Katie on the beach was all I needed to see to know that she was having the time of her life. The smile on her face, from ear to ear was priceless, and I knew that we overcame a challenged poised to us. People with disabilities are faced with difficult situations, but by finding the power and courage to overcome them, anybody can do accomplish anything. Siblings of disabled kids can live normal lives, and do anything and everything their peers do. It just takes a little resilience.

Disabilities come in all different types of shapes and sizes. From debilitating muscular diseases, to speech difficulties or autism; disabilities spread among a large horizon. With these disabilities come the facts that people simply cannot do some things that others can. People are unable to do it. Sadly, people place such a large emphasis on what people cannot do. People seem to worry more about what

people cannot do than finding what one can do. The negative attitude focuses too much on the can not's, and not enough on the cans.

Growing up with my siblings, I too, have seen this first hand
where people quickly look at the negatives without seeing a positive.
The difficulties are placed first, and there is no effort to find what one
can successfully do. As a sibling to people with disabilities, I always
saw people saying no to Katie and Robert. No, you can't walk. No,
you can't talk clearly. No, you cannot read a college textbook. No,
you cannot provide anything special to this planet.

Well, I have news for all of you. Katie and Robert, and people
with disabilities provide more for this world than anybody else ever
could. Their gifts and talents are so numerous that one cannot simply
ever grasp what they are receiving from people with disabilities. In
my eyes, people do not have disabilities, but rather people's abilities
are just different. The world places too much emphasis on disabilities
without seeing people's various different abilities.

Growing up with my siblings, I have been able to focus on their
abilities and forget all that they cannot do. Take Robert, for example.
There is not one place I can go with him that he does not know somebody. From his engagements through sports, he has met so many
people and left an impact on so many lives. I am always so humbled
and happy to hear people out in public tell me that Robert is "the
best," or that Robert is "the man." I always joke that Robert is like a
mayor, because everybody in the town knows him by first name, and
to him they are all his friends.

Sure, Robert has suffered from many different things. His fine
motor skills are weak, and his vision is not perfect. But, he is one
of the friendliest people I know with a heart the size of the world.
People could focus on his disabilities, but if they did, they would all

that he has to offer the world. He is the definition of charismatic, and the world has taken notice.

Similarly to Robert, Katie has also can do so much that people need to see how moving forward in life can make her smile through tears. Last summer at Young Life Camp, Katie did something that I will remember for the rest of my life. She went on the giant swing. For those of you not familiar with the giant swing, the giant swing is a big swing that people harness in to and ride in many different Young Life Camps around the country.

It was a typical Arizona afternoon when the time came for our group to go on the swing. We arrived at the site, and harnessed up all of the people who wanted to ride. It wasn't just the able bodied kids who could ride the swing, anybody could. Katie took up this offer like nobody else.

The last time Katie was on a swing she was probably seven years old at the park running around with her friends. This time, she was in a wheelchair and still jumping at the bit to go on an even bigger swing.

Katie was harnessed up, and then tied up on the swing next to my mother and another Young Life leader. The swing rose, and she was about to go on a ride. Not wanting to do too big of a jolt, the swing was only raised about half way up. Man, was that still very high. My mom pulled the release, then off the three went swinging in the air. Katie was having the time of her life. After an initial scared look from the first drop, a smile then erupted across her face and she was able to enjoy the swinging ride. She loved every minute of it.

I never would have guessed that Katie would go on that swing. I never dreamt that she would want to and she would be able to. With the amazing support of the Young Life staff, and the immense amount of courage displayed by Katie, she did it and loved every minute of it. Katie defied the odds, and did what many probably think she'd never do. That is smiling through tears. That is being resilient and moving on forward with your life.

Growing up with my siblings I saw many difficult situations arise where people either doubted my siblings' abilities to do something, or focused on their disabilities. Despite also seeing how their difficulties made doing some things very complicated; I later found that they could do anything they put their mind to. Growing up with my siblings, I learned the importance of resilience and the fact that despite tears holding one back, by focusing on the good and finding everyone's abilities, everyone can smile.

No disability is too great for one to be able to live a successful life, and despite doing things a little differently at times, siblings of children with debilities can live lives similar to that of their peers, but with a little extra passion for what they are doing. Setbacks will come up in your journey, but with the strength of God; you can smile through any tear.

It was tears for my entire family seeing my sister go through all of her challenges, and it was tears for my family when my brother was in emergency surgery as a baby. It was tears in our eyes, and it is tears that many people shed when life throws us curveballs. What comes with difficult circumstances is also a choice. A choice to let the devastation win, and overthrow your life, or a choice to tackle the adversity, find the meaning behind it all, and smile knowing God is holding your hand along the way. Be resilient as you overcome your challenges, and always smile through the tears.

12

Somebody for Me

"The best love is the one that makes you a better person,
without changing you into someone other than yourself."
- Unknown

$\mathcal{E}$very child dreams of finding true love and riding away in a carriage. It is something engrained in all of us by Disney movies and tradition: a young girl's dream of finding Prince Charming, a man who will love them unconditionally and keep them safe. Boys, on the other hand, dream of finding a Princess who will help them go through life successfully, and take on life's bumps by their side.

What happens when you grow up with siblings with special needs? Do the healthy siblings still have the same dreams and aspirations as their peers? Normally, when a couple enters a relationship, they get used to each other's "baggage and bad habits," and then continue on in their relationship focusing on the good.

So, what happens though, when there is actual baggage? Like two siblings with special needs who someday will be under your care and supervision, and who frequently require extra help and are immensely involved in your life. How do you explain that baggage to a prospective suitor? Do you inform your significant other about your siblings at the beginning of the relationship? Do you brush over it and not mention it until the relationship gets stronger? How do you share the life that you actually live in a way that makes you feel accepted and understood?

Growing up, I struggled with these questions because I did not know the best way to share my situation with others. I did not know how to introduce girlfriends, just friends who were girls, or even just friends in general to my siblings. I was especially worried that girls would shy away from me because of my siblings, and I was concerned that girls would simply look past me because of the extra weight I carried. In middle school and high school when we had school dances, I never brought my siblings with me to pictures and events related to the dances because I was simply embarrassed and concerned that I would be judged by my dates because of my siblings.

I hate to look back on this, but it gave me great worry thinking about what others would think of me and my siblings. I love my siblings to death, but I wanted to shield them and myself from the negative situations which could arise with others' ignorance. Siblings of children with disabilities face many unique challenges in their lives. This harsh reality may cause many healthy siblings to live in fear of rejection and isolation.

Despite that, the greatest sorrow I felt from growing up came with the realization of indifference in our world. A majority of our society does not feel any empathy or compassion towards people in need or who are marginalized. The 21st century lifestyle of greed, and the search for wealth, has pushed people away from being concerned about others and caring about people's different needs and wants. This tragedy is the propeller around my worry of acceptance among my peers and potential significant others. How can I impress someone with the life I lived where nothing is *ever* perfect?

With people so focused on being better than everybody else, the fear of not being the best kept me hindered in my search for others. Our society's culture inevitably forces a situation where people simply miss out on love for one another for who they truly are. By focusing on ourselves, we simply look past some of God's very best people. If we just stop and dig a little deeper into each others' lives, we will open our hearts to the unique and wonderful people who make up our world.

All of my fears of finding a girl who would accept my situation disappeared the summer before my freshman year at Santa Clara University. Young Life Capernaum, a ministry I volunteer for in San Jose, takes campers to a week long summer camp every year in Williams, Arizona. The camp, Lost Canyon, is nestled in the Arizona forest with a zip-line, swing and horse barn, a pool with water slides, and resort style lodging and dining.

For one week, people with special needs from all over the country experience God and love in one great place by being surrounded by kids like themselves and leaders and volunteers who selflessly devote themselves to giving the kids the time of their life like they truly deserve. For a whole week, friends with disabilities make best friends from all over the world and share in fellowship and good company as they hear The Word and see the good in all of our lives with Christ. The camp is truly a remarkable time to see people with disabilities overcome their fears and worries and just enjoy life and meet new, life-long friends as all people at the camp have the sole mission of sharing God with everybody and being his servants on this land.

The camp week was an emotional rollercoaster for me. For one, I was leading the boys for the first time on my own. I was finally a legal adult, so Adan, another leader who is in a wheelchair and I headed up the boy's cabin and strived to show the Lord to our friends. For that, I was a little nervous. Secondly, my sister came to camp this week with my mom. The smile on Katie's face was immense the whole week, and I had never seen her as happy as she was than at that week at camp. For this, I was overflowed with joy. Finally, though, for which I am most grateful; I met an amazing young girl who opened my eyes to the belief that there are girls in our world who will look past all of my extra baggage and view me for the person I am. For this, my life found new hope. That was amazing.

Our group of kids with special needs was paired up with five girls from Jackson, Mississippi. They were volunteering their time at the camp to give their love to others. They belong to a Young Life club in Jackson, but this week they shared their love of God with kids with special needs. Throughout the week, I witnessed the girls fully giving themselves to others, and making our friends with special needs feel loved and desired.

Over the course of the week though; I watched one girl in particular devote her time to others and display God's love to all. Makenna; a brown haired, green eyed, southern accented, beautiful young woman, selflessly served these amazing kids. From throwing water balloons with my sister at me, to listening to stories of our friends lives, to playing games with all of our campers; Makenna showed me how special some people are when they fully give themselves to others. She displayed what it meant to be a selfless person. From helping people at different activities, to consoling some friends who were upset, to praying with people who were in need; she put her personal needs aside and helped those in need. Makenna did not care who she was with; she was just the hands and feet of Christ and selflessly gave herself to all of the kids at camp.

The week progressed, and as Makenna and I became acquainted; I started developing a little crush. She was very cute and kind, so it was natural to start developing some feelings. Who can blame me? I know what you are all thinking; "summertime love." Well yes, that could be argued, but I believed that our relationship had a chance of becoming a deep and lasting one.

The week moved on and I was continuously impressed by the size of Makenna's heart. It is the biggest in the world. Sadly though, I did not give Makenna any hints that I thought she was cute and that I had a crush on her. I figured that she lived in Jackson, Mississippi (over 2000 miles away per her calculations), and that I should not fall too hard for a girl who I might never see again. Although, when western night came, I made sure we got a cute picture together for memories which I could remember forever.

The week flew by and I was disappointed in thinking that she would be departing forever. It was a sad realization, but, nonetheless, the night came when she and her fellow buddies had to leave to go back to Mississippi. We enjoyed our final night together and then, as I was walking back to my cabin, I heard Makenna yell "Bye, Michael!" I turned around and saw her standing in front of the club room. I then walked back to give her a hug goodbye. (Let me remind you that I still believed that I had a crush on her and would never see her again and that she was just being friendly saying goodbye.) So, we said our goodbyes and went our separate ways.

The following day; I texted Makenna just to say hello. She had already put her phone number into my phone so I could send her a picture. To my luck, she texted me back and we started talking. All day long. We talked about the memories we shared at camp, as well as other topics which were on our minds. Man, did we connect. As I talked with her, I felt like I had known her for a hundred years. We instantly connected on a deeper level and we created a mutual bond very quickly.

Over the next few days, our relationship grew. We kept learning more and more about each other and expressed some feelings toward one another. Then, Makenna blew up my world. She started complimenting me and talking kindly about me. Yes, kind of in a flirtatious way. She told me how she, too, had a little crush at camp on me. I did not believe her at first, but she joked about different times when her friends tried to make it obvious to me, yet I remained oblivious. (Yes, I must admit now that boys are oblivious to a lot.) I was in disbelief. I did not know what to think besides the fact that I was talking to one of the greatest persons I had ever met.

Makenna opened my heart in a way that nobody else ever had. She was put in my life at the perfect time, and her impact on my life was only beginning. Her love for God and serving others was beyond evident, and I know that her faith and mine is what drew us close together. Besides, who would think that an 18 year old boy from California would develop strong feelings for a 17 year old girl from Mississippi? And vice versa? It was truly propelled by a greater power, despite us falling into a great relationship on our own.

As I continued talking to Makenna, I told her about things in my life that I had never shared with anybody else. I opened up my life to her because I knew in my heart that she would understand. She made me feel like nobody else ever had. I told her about some of my concerns about opening my heart to her because of the fears I felt she might have about my siblings. Her response melted my heart. She responded, "I would never run away from Katie or anything in your life." I had told her how other girls had been shy and afraid of my situation, but Makenna cured my heart and assured me that she would look at me as the person I was. Makenna said that is what attracted her to me in the first place. The words uttered from her mouth were words I had lost sleep about for years on end. I just needed to hear somebody speak the words she spoke. Man, did she make my life by saying it. You see, everybody dreams of finding someone who makes their life spin in the right direction, and Makenna, being her own wonderful self, assured me that I was worthy of finding happiness in a relationship with a wonderful woman.

Makenna and I continued to talk on the phone, and we learned more and more about each other. It was a great time we had, learning about each other's lives. We had an instant connection and bonded immediately. The quickness and the intensity of our feelings towards each other are hard to explain to others, but Makenna and I understood it all completely; and that's all that really mattered.

After about a week being home from camp, my life took another unexpected turn. Katie got very sick. She spiked a high fever of 101 degrees, and was severely congested in the respiratory system. She went to the doctor and was given antibiotics and began to get better. After five days on antibiotics, she spiked a fever of 103 degrees. My mom took her back to the doctor and the doctor sent her straight to the Emergency Room, suspecting Sepsis. Katie's blood pressure and pulse were very high. The nurse hooked her up to an IV and then Katie had blood taken. The lab results showed that she had a high lactic acid count and a high white blood cell count. The hospital called a code Shock Alert on her and the nurse explained that now she would be getting all her tests and care STAT. The Shock Alert team was working very quickly to make sure Katie got the care she needed quickly. Minutes count when a patient is diagnosed with Sepsis. Wow, was this a scare.

I was very concerned about Katie, but for the first time in my life, I opened up about the situation to someone not in my family. Makenna just felt like the person who I could talk to about it openly and freely. Throughout my life, I have often kept these situations to myself and did not vent to anybody, but for some reason, Makenna was the person I knew I could talk to. Was I ever right! She loved on me like no other friend ever had. Every day she asked me how Katie was doing, and asked if I needed to talk about anything. I was home alone for a few days, and each night she called me to cheer me up and just talk about my day.

It was something I looked forward to each night. Her compassion and attention was immeasurable and it meant the world to me. Makenna's concern and support of me and my family lifted my worries and comforted me deeply. I remember talking to Makenna one night and she told me that "She wished she could be at the hospital with Katie even when I was gone and busy at work." Who says that? If you are not smiling right now from ear to ear; I doubt your attention to detail. Because this; love from Makenna was truly inspirational.

For the first time in my life, I found someone who viewed me for the person I was, but at the same time viewed Katie, as Katie. Throughout various different situations, people viewed Katie as a wheelchair. It was the first thing they saw when they saw her, so immediately that is what she was. Not Makenna. Makenna saw Katie as the same beautiful young girl that I see. Makenna was blinded from the differences, but bound by the perfect person Katie was.

This is what I cherish the most about Makenna. I feared for so long that I would never be able to find someone to see Katie the way I saw her. I feared that no one would break down barriers to find the perfect being my sister was. Makenna took away that fear. Makenna saw Katie as the amazing girl she is, and this made me rest assured knowing I too could be accepted for the life I was in. Makenna didn't care that I lived a unique life, she saw me for who I was, and that is what she liked. I am a very lucky guy.

I was at home one afternoon after work changing before going to the hospital and I noticed a beautiful flower arrangement on the porch. I didn't have any idea who they were from, but I know, you guessed it. Yes, Makenna sent them. What an amazing girl. Her concern for Katie from so far away was a beautiful thing to witness. Man, did it make me like her even more! Makenna is truly one in a million and I cannot tell you how she makes me feel. She puts me in a place of contentment and satisfaction that I have never been in before.

Well, if you are interested in the rest of the story of Makenna and me, the story is still being written. I have a flight booked to visit her next month, and I cannot wait to see where we go. I know that God is behind this relationship one hundred percent, and she and I both trust that He will lead us in our relationship. I just cannot wait to enjoy memories together and see what we can accomplish with each other by our sides.

The difficult questions in life of who you are going to build strong relationships with and share your life with are difficult for anybody. But the life I live made me question my life's future even more. I just was not confident that I would ever find someone who would be completely comfortable in my situation. Through relationships with some people, I knew that it would be difficult to find a person who would be comfortable living life by my side.

I don't blame them because many people are just not familiar with many things that are inevitable in my life. Besides their ignorance; I was still unsure if anybody would ever fill the shoes I needed filled. Makenna's arrival in my life was a pivotal moment and it answered so many prayers and questions. I cannot tell you how her presence lifted my heart and opened my eyes to a whole new world. I can never give back to her the confidence and assurance she gave me.

Siblings of children with disabilities face special conditions. They face many extra hurdles that their peers do not. Through Makenna's arrival in my life; I am now confident that there are people in our world who are open to all and base their relationships on love, and love only. I do not know what Makenna's and my future holds; only God knows what our plan is to be. I pray we have a long-lasting relationship where we can help each other through life's challenges. I know we both will actively pursue our relationship together, but in the end, only time will tell what our future holds.

Despite this though, Makenna has opened my life to a whole new perspective. I am now confident that our world holds special people who love unconditionally and use it to propel their relationships with others. Makenna has been a testament to my new belief, and I have learned that siblings of children with disabilities do not need to fear rejection or isolation from others. There are people in our world who simply love.

Proverbs 27:17 says, "As iron sharpens iron, so a friend sharpens a friend." We can all benefit from other people in our lives. We can become better people though if we find someone who can work with us and provide us with endless love. Good people in your life make you better. Makenna has been someone who has made me a better person. She has strengthened my relationship with God, and she has shown me that if we look in all the right places, amazing people will come into your life. I know that siblings of people with disabilities desire and need the strength of others in their life to make them better people. Makenna has proved to me that there are people in our world who see past any differences, and love you simply for who you are. It is my wish that you too can find the person in your life that you can lean on in times of need, celebrate with in times of joy, and love for being there for you in every situation.

When starting a relationship with someone, it is important to be completely open. People deserve to know what they are getting into, and it is essential in building a strong, lasting bond. In our world today, we are so connected that nothing can remain hidden. Thus, issues such as the aforementioned are important to discuss in a relationship because they do not distance people, but only bring them closer together. It gives people more tolerance and understanding. Above all, it gives us hope for the world of tomorrow.

Being open from the beginning is the only way to start a relationship because from what I have learned from Makenna, some people in our world do understand people's differences. They are existent in our lives. Sometimes you just have to dig far and dig deep to find them. As the quote from the beginning of the chapter states, we must find people in our lives who love us just the way we are, and who have no interest in changing our ways. When one can find someone who takes them just the way they are, it is important to pursue that other being. That is the kind of love that will prevail through all of life's challenges. Makenna opened my eyes to the world of possibility, and from her I have learned that being myself and opening my unique life to others is the best way to create a lasting bond. It is my wish that siblings of children with disabilities can find their "Makenna" and feel comfortable being themselves.

Well, the stories Walt Disney and his crew wrote are stories that can exist for all. Everybody can find someone who loves them for who they are, and together they can ride away happily ever after. I feared for so long that people would not love me for the person I was, but instead would fear the different life I lived. I now know that people like Makenna are in our world, and are ready to love one another unconditionally and focus on each other's good, positive characteristics. Siblings of children with disabilities deserve to find a significant other who can help them overcome various different challenges. They deserve a shoulder to lean on, and other to love them back. Opening your life to others can be insanely hard; it is tough to let down your guard. In the end, however, by doing so, you will find a satisfaction in the world that you never felt before. Your heart will feel full. I'm just glad I found Makenna to show me this love. Because I now know that there is somebody for me.

13

Finding his Footprints

"However bad life may seem, there is always something you can do, and succeed at. While there's life, there is hope."
- Stephen Hawking

" *J*esus replied, 'You do not realize now what I am doing, but later you will understand.'" John 13:7

Many times in our lives we face a situation which makes us freeze and think about why the situation is occurring. It is common for people to encounter difficult situations and not clearly understand it at all. I can vow for that, but if we dig into scripture and read His word in the aforementioned verse, we can see how Jesus believes that from each trial there can be revealed a reason after undergoing the difficult circumstance. Jesus proclaims that after the tribulation occurs, some greater understanding will be uncovered that explains why the hardship had to occur.

After undergoing the life of growing up with siblings with special needs, I have found a greater understanding for understanding why I was placed into the situation. After finding Christ in my life and seeing all that he provides, an understanding of why it all happened to me was revealed. There are many tough questions that arise when growing up with siblings with special needs, but from finding the grace of God and seeing his footprints in my life, I now have a greater understanding of why everything occurred the way that it did.

Challenges face everybody every day. The challenges may be hard to comprehend at first, but if you find the giving grace in it and accept the situation, you will better be able to comprehend the reasoning for why it had to exist and have a better understanding of why it happened to you.

I believe that there are some lessons in life that you simply cannot learn unless you go through something traumatic or life changing. So, to me, you take a situation that appears to be bad or dire or even life-changing, and you look back at it after a few years and you can say, you know I've learned some lessons in life that could never be taught in a million years, no matter how much kind of set up went into it. The lessons learned and the new information attained can provide you in your life a new vision and a new future. The lessons can give you a new path for your life and point you in the direction you are supposed to go down. Finding God's footprints in your life and with you in your challenges will help you understand the challenges you face, and give you the strength and fortitude to overcome anything you ever encounter.

It was the fall of 2015, and my parents had just moved me into my dorm at Santa Clara University. We had my clothes put away, the bed made, and the other goods placed in their respective locations. I was ready to start my college life. Before I could start the new adventure, there was one more thing we had to get: a fan. The dorms were without air-conditioning and it was almost 100 degrees that day. Boy, did we need a fan.

My parents left me at school and drove back home to grab a portable fan at the house. In the meantime, I met some new friends and started learning as much as I could about my new home. A few hours later, I got a call from my mom and she told me that she had just arrived to the school with my fan. I left my room and walked down the short flight of stairs from the second floor. I walked outside, and there in the car was my mom, sister, and the dog. I went and grabbed the fan and said goodbye, but before I could leave, my mom told me to sit down in the front seat for a quick second. I assumed it was going to be some lecture on making smart decisions or about studying, etc., but no, it was more than that.

My mom sat me down and looked me in the eye and uttered these exact words, "Michael, I want you to go, spread your horizons and find your footprints in this community. You are just as good as anyone else at this school, and I want you to be happy and satisfied in this new community. I love you! Go show people who you are, people will take notice."

Wow. What a lecture from Mom that was. I did the typical teenage move and nodded my head and acted like I already knew what she was saying. After I got out of the car and started walking back to my room, a tear rolled right down my face. Her words struck me just the right way, and for the rest of my life, I guarantee you I will remember that very conversation. It was great motherly advice, and it was something that gave me an immense amount of confidence and direction.

Moving away from home to college is a big step in growing-up. Whether it is twenty-five miles away from home, or two thousand, it is a big step which takes a lot of courage and strength. Every year, thousands of 18 year olds pack their bags and step foot in a new community with no grounding or bearings. They are set in loose sand with a need to find their own footprints in a new community.

Finding your place in a new society and community can be hard. It takes a lot of courage to meet new, unfamiliar faces, and the lack of knowing people you are now living with makes the transition even more difficult. So my mom's words gave me some courage to find my place at my new school. It may be hard at times, but with the right foundation and confidence, every other student and I alike, can find their place in their new school community.

Now, you may be wondering what about my transition into college has to do with the rest of my book. The truth of the matter is, just like new students have to find their footprints in college, siblings of children with disabilities have to find their own footprints in the world. Everyone has to find their place in the world, but siblings of children with disabilities especially need to find their place as it will give them meaning and purpose to fulfill the life they have been given. They need to find their own footprints where they feel full and satisfied.

"What is my purpose? What am I supposed to do?" I remember one day talking to Makenna after she had just received some difficult news. She was to be facing a new battle, but had the courage and passion as big as I have ever seen to overcome this tribulation. When trying to explain how she accepted it, she said that it was a way of God telling her where she needed to focus her life. She was certain that her purpose on this earth was to help others, and her reasoning made me think of why I too had to undergo difficult circumstances and what I was supposed to do from it. Our two trials are completely different, but nonetheless they both are adversities that have to be overcome.

This situation led me to think of why I too was on this earth. What was my destiny?

Siblings of children with disabilities gain invaluable experience about helping others. They are constantly in situations where they have to give up their own wants and needs and instead do everything in their power to give themselves to others; to be selfless. So what was God thinking when he gave me my life? He doesn't want pain and suffering, but looking deeper into each situation; God is teaching us something through it, and we need to grasp and accept it for what it is. What exactly is it that God is teaching me, and wanting me to do?

Well, in my life, I have always found joy in volunteering with various organizations and finding ways to help others in need. It makes me happy helping others. Maybe God gave me these skills to go inspire the world. I know there is some intervention in my life from Him for sure. Further, I could argue that God wanted me to write this book to reach other's lives who are too often finding themselves quiet and isolated. God works wonders through us, and if we stop to notice it, we all can see what God is doing through us.

Regardless though of what I feel God has planned for me to do, I do know I was put on this planet to help others and spread the love of God to people who have every reason not to see it. When I truly, down-right accepted God into my life at the age of seventeen, I, for the first time, felt that God's hand was on me and my siblings for eternity. For so long I could not believe that God would want pain to damage lives; I couldn't see a divine presence when so many people close to me were suffering so much. I just could not understand God being in control over lives in pain, but after I prayed, spent time in worship with others, and saw the grace of God in my siblings' lives, I found a new sense of direction and purpose. I found my footprints, when God's were there with me.

Siblings of children with disabilities more often than not grow up and embark on careers which focus around helping others. Extended family members also have a high rate of finding ways to give back to people in need, but studies have shown that siblings have a very high rate of assistance-oriented careers. They feel that they are called to be an influential person who upholds the dignity of others, and thus they find vocations which assist others. In my opinion, after growing up in my situation, I feel like it is an obligation to give back to people who have given you so much.

My family has been blessed by doctors, donors, friends, family, and strangers alike. So I personally feel that it is now my job to give back to others the love and help that we received. This belief of mine is shared by so many people, and it is a great thing to see as we find many people doing wonderful things in our world and helping people who need it the most. I remember at times people would ask me why I went and donated time at Young Life, or collected and donated pumpkin pies at Thanksgiving for homeless mothers. They just didn't understand my desire or passion for helping others. At the same time, I found my place where I could find humility and purpose. My heart was full by doing so. I was fulfilling my destiny.

Siblings of children of disabilities may have their heart strings pulled in a way different than that of their peers, but understand that there is a deeper reason you are feeling the way you are, and it is ok. Embrace it and follow your heart. Find your footprints on this planet and love the life you want to live. Whether you become a pastor who preaches the gospel, a doctor who volunteers his or her services in parts of the developing world, a teacher who imprints knowledge on the generation of tomorrow, a volunteer helping in charitable organizations, or a public official who strives to create positive change for the greater world, understand that your experiences from your unique perspective will change the world forever. Your knowledge is greater than anything else in the world. You are in this world with your vision for a distinct reason, so encompass your destiny and leave an everlasting impact on this planet.

Life's barriers are strong, and they are wide, but they are very penetrable. Every barrier we face in our lives can be transformed into a door to something far greater than we ever could have imagined. I wouldn't ever have imagined the amazing gifts I have received from my siblings. It isn't always noticeable at first sight, but after the acceptance of the challenge and the realization that something more is trying to reveal itself, hidden blessings can be uncovered through any circumstance. It just takes time to understand them.

I do not know what challenges are going to arise in your life. I do not know which obstacles you are going to face on your life's journeys. But what I do know is that through each and every trial and tribulation you face, you will gain something far greater than you ever could have imagined. Each difficult situation you engage in will reveal a new hidden blessing; you just have to work to uncover it.

As I finish this book, it is my wish that you take away a new sense of purpose and direction as you work to find your own footprints through life's challenges. I write this with great humility, and I hope that you are able to find some solace and hope that comes from the Lord when it seems like life's hurdles are never ending.

Let me leave you with my favorite verse from the Bible. Hebrews 12: 1-2 reads, "Therefore, since we are surrounded by so great a cloud of witnesses, let us also lay aside every weight, and sin which clings so closely, and let us run with endurance the race that is set before us, looking to Jesus, the founder and perfecter of our faith, who for the joy that was set before him endured the cross, despising the shame, and is seated at the right hand of the throne of God."

My wish is that you find His footprints in your life, but more importantly, you find your footprints in His life. Each and every sibling of children with disabilities faces a unique life, but nonetheless it is their life, and they are in it for a reason. Go make your footprints in this world. I guarantee you that people will see them, acknowledge your tracks, and find hope.

With your new sense of love and hope, live your life with purpose and meaning. I pray we all feel the company of Christ in our lives, and that we use our purpose and destiny to go touch the world and spread His message of hope and love to all of the land.

A final word from Michael

*a*s I conclude this book, I find myself sitting in a place far too familiar to me and my family; a hospital chair. Once again, actually for the third time in two months, Katie is in the hospital with lactic acid buildup, a high white blood count, and a rather huge fever. Doctors can't seem to locate an infection, but nonetheless she is being prescribed medications and fluids to try and get her situation under control. Again, I find myself in the hospital watching my sibling undergo so much that she does not deserve, unsure of why all of this has to happen. The obstacles simply keep arising, and the challenges never seize to disappear.

You see, even after one can find solace and acceptance as to why challenges in their life have to occur, one will continuously still be tried by the unimaginable. Even after finding a saving grace, such as God, the persistent challenges that overcome peoples' lives will still occur and test their faith time and time again. As I sit here and write this, I trust that God is in control and that His hand is on the situation. But, I must admit that as I drove over here to the hospital tonight from my school, I also had all of the emotions I had felt before finding my footprints as to why this had to happen to my sibling, and also why

I had to deal with this as the healthy sibling. I strongly believe that God's hand is on the situation, but my emotions and faith are still constantly tried as each day brings new challenges.

Siblings of children with disabilities face never-ending battles. Just when life looks like it is going smooth, within a blink of an eye the unfathomable can occur. That is one of the great challenges siblings face. These trials test the healthy siblings time and time again, but as I too face the challenges time and time again; the faith I have always prevails and comforts me in these moments of distress.

Difficult situations are still going to arise after finding God in your life and in your situation; He is not going to stop them. Trials will keep arising and try to rip your faith right from your hand. By holding to the principles of your faith and trusting in it no matter the circumstances, the challenges you face will slowly diminish and your ability to overcome them will greatly increase.

Finding His footprints in your life is very important as it paves a way for you to find your footprints in His life. The hope you gain is irreplaceable, and your future is so much brighter. No matter what you may encounter, the hope you have for tomorrow will outweigh any fear you have for today.

It is my wish that each sunrise brings you new hope, and that each sunset gives you peace in the day. So as I leave you, I say to you, have hope in your life, and trust that there is a plan already written for you. By doing so, you will accomplish the unthinkable, and overcome any challenge you may face.

Thank you for opening your heart to my story, and may God bless you all.

Michael John Deauville

CPSIA information can be obtained
at www.ICGtesting.com
Printed in the USA
LVOW06s1056120916

504238LV00005B/21/P